Collecting Marine Tropicals

RODNEY JONKLAAS

© T.F.H. Publications, Inc.

Distributed in the UNITED STATES to the Pet Trade by T.F.H. Publications, Inc., 1 TFH Plaza, Neptune City, NJ 07753; on the Internet at www.tfh.com; in CANADA by Rolf C. Hagen Inc., 3225 Sartelon St., Montreal, Quebec H4R 1E8; Pet Trade by H & L Pet Supplies Inc., 27 Kingston Crescent, Kitchener, Ontario N2B 2T6; in ENGLAND by T.F.H. Publications, PO Box 74, Havant PO9 5TT; in AUSTRALIA AND THE SOUTH PACIFIC by T.F.H. (Australia), Pty. Ltd., Box 149, Brookvale 2100 N.S.W., Australia; in NEW ZEALAND by Brooklands Aquarium Ltd., 5 McGiven Drive, New Plymouth, RD1 New Zealand; in SOUTH AFRICA by Rolf C. Hagen S.A. (PTY.) LTD., P.O. Box 201199, Durban North 4016, South Africa; in JAPAN by T.F.H. Publications. Published by T.F.H. Publications, Inc.

MANUFACTURED IN THE
UNITED STATES OF AMERICA
BY T.F.H. PUBLICATIONS, INC.

Rodney Jonklaas collecting anemonefishes with a hand net while SCUBA diving in Sri Lanka. Photo by Dr. Herbert R. Axelrod.

After several years of cajoling, Dr. Herbert Axelrod, with whom I have spent many hours collecting tropicals off Sri Lanka and the Maldives, has persuaded me to write this book.

"If you don't, someone else will," said Herbert.

So here it is, for what it is worth to professionals, amateurs and general readers.

There are many secrets in this book and, no doubt, professionals who have treasured them will take me to task for having revealed them. On the other hand, I feel that it is better to reveal safe and humane techniques in the interests of conservation than to permit novices to experiment, as I did, and in the process unnecessarily cause the demise of some of Earth's most gorgeous living creatures.

I have considerable experience in the areas of India, Sri Lanka, the Maldives and the South China Sea off the coast of Malaysia. Undoubtedly, additional techniques other than mine and unknown to me prevail elsewhere.

This book primarily is concerned with the smaller marine fishes and invertebrates and not the very large specimens collected for public aquariums. The fishes described are, for the most part, less than a foot in length; and many of them are less than four inches, which is the most commonly sought-after size by professionals like me for the thriving marine tropicals business.

The main theme of this work centers around diving techniques to collect marines. Other methods are reasonably effective, but for obtaining most of the choice specimens economically and in good condition, one must

Collecting jars to store collected animals make it unnecessary for a diver to constantly return to the surface to unload the catch. Photo by Jerry Greenberg.

be something of a diver, and if trained in SCUBA, so much the better.

Stress is placed also on economy of space, energy, expenditures and time. I have endeavored to present the most effective and economical method of collecting a specific fish. If expense and time were of no concern, this book hardly would be worth reading. One who is very rich can quite easily

empty gallons of a soporific chemical into a body of water and happily collect the stunned specimens he wants. This emphatically is not what I want to happen anywhere in the world. It is the most callous and wasteful form of fishing known. It is even more insidious than the use of explosives.

Even by starting marine fish collecting the hard way, and still being engaged in it many years later, I cannot boast yet that every fish I would like to capture alive is at my mercy. I am still learning and experimenting and, no doubt, when I cannot dive actively any longer, there still may be several elusive lovelies which someone else will learn to collect more effectively than I.

CONSERVATION IN GENERAL

It is an unhappy but real enough situation which indicates that, as every day goes by the shallower seas of the world are being depleted of their fauna. Conservationists are hard at work trying to stem the decimation of certain species and postpone the inevitable. The subject is an enormous one, and the collection of live tropical marines and invertebrates forms a very tiny fraction of it.

There are people who are wont to lay blame on collectors only for depopulating reefs and rocky coastlines of the more attractive and exotic small fauna. This is hardly fair when one stops to consider the tremendous damage done to fishes, big and small, by the commercial fishermen who seek fish for food.

However diligently and successfully a team of divers may work over a coral reef, the catch they make will not compare with a single haul of a beach seine in adjacent waters.

The fact remains that skillful collectors do make an

Seines are useful for collecting fishes over sandy or grassy bottoms. Sea horses and pipefishes are usually captured in this manner. Photo by M. D. Bellomy.

impression on a coral reef. Reefs certainly deserve protection, but not just from marine tropical collectors. If a body of water is to be protected, then by all means do so, but keep all forms of fishing out of it!

I am reminded of the peculiar situation in the John Pennekamp National Park off Florida, where spearfishermen were forbidden to operate, but commercial fishermen with nets and lines were! Hardly a National Park!

Even in unprotected areas, collectors are ill-advised to go all out and catch every speci-

men of a rare fish they can see. There are a good many marine species which do not breed prolifically enough to keep pace with systematic collecting, or whose fry survival percentage is too low. Many of the species listed have not yet revealed details of their breeding habits. A fair number of them can be exterminated totally from a particular area.

The fact that a fish of Indo-Pacific distribution is never numerous anywhere, but is widespread, indicates that it lays very few eggs or that the survival rate of fry is low. On the other hand, the fact that a species is never found in concentrations may indicate that its habits are solitary or strongly territorial as mated pairs. To collect such fish too indiscriminately could lead to quite large areas being denuded of the species.

As a professional, in the past 20 years of collecting I have seen with dismay the diminution of beautiful fishes

off the reefs of Sri Lanka, Malaysia and parts of India. However well-stocked a coral reef may seem, a large proportion of the more attractive fishes can be reduced visibly by intensive collecting.

Here are a few of the marine gems from Sri Lanka which face grave danger of extermination from these waters:

The clown trigger (*Balistoides conspicillum*), the blue grouper (*Epinephelus flavocoeruleus*), the imperial angel (*Pomacanthus imperator*), the regal tang (*Paracanthurus hepatus*), the longnose butterflyfish (*Forcipiger flavissimus*), the saddleback butterfly (*Chaetodon ephippium*) and a few others. The marine collectors are not to be blamed fully for this. Very many rare fishes are killed for food by net, trap, line and (sadly) dynamite fishermen.

It is the same, if not worse,

Sometimes collecting is interrupted by a curious "spectator" like this Jewfish (*Epinephelus itajara*) and picture taking then commences. Photo by Mike Mesgleski.

in other countries. In Malaysia, in the South China Sea, I dove off the remotest islands and found them sadly depleted of most species which were at one time abundant. In these places, it was not the

A large wrasse "poses" for its portrait as surgeonfishes swim past in the background.

Photo courtesy Jim & Cathy Church.

At public aquariums crowds are attracted by divers working with dangerous sea creatures like this Green Moray (*Gymnothorax funebris*). These eels can even be coaxed out of their hiding places.

Photo by Raphael Mesa.

tropical marine collectors who were responsible, but the professional trap and line fishermen. For instance, it was appalling to see little boys with simple goggles hunting butterflyfishes for food armed with Hawaiian-sling type harpoon-guns!

The live-bait collectors for the skipjack and tuna fishing industries of Sri Lanka and the Maldives regularly harvest huge numbers of pomacentrids, butterflyfishes, anthids and labrids, which are used for bait or chum. In the deep ocean where they are dumped, it is certain that hardly any survive.

It may be wishful thinking at this stage that sometime in the near future a far-seeing government of some tropical country may formulate legislation to protect and conserve tropical marine fishes. Also, they could economically and conserva-tively harvest these fishes for aquariums and still make a profit. The last scheme is feasible. Indeed, it has been tried out on a small scale off Sri Lanka by collectors like me. By sparing some and harvesting a proportion of young marines, by eliminating over-grown and non-breeding resident "bullies," reefs that still are unknown to the more ruthless collectors remain fertile collecting grounds year after year.

If done in the proper manner, moray eels, here a Green Moray (*Gymnothorax funebris*), can be handled without harm to the handler or the fish. Do not try this unless you are an expert, morays are very dangerous!

Photo by Raphael Mesa.

A Short History of My Marine Fish Collecting Off Sri Lanka

Several years ago, Hugh Stewart and I were diving with masks off the coast of Colombo. Around a sunken piece of angle iron, standing upright on a shallow, murky bottom, were two elegant little fish with white pennant-like dorsals.

"We must catch those little Irish Models!", gasped Hugh.

And catch them we did, the next day, with home-made nets. It took us two hours to net the elusive, little juvenile Pennant Butterflyfish (*Heniochus acuminatus*). The first Moorish Idols (Hugh's Irish Models) were collected a few years later. From that memorable day onward, I devoted a greater part of my underwater activity to collecting marines.

Later on, I accompanied the first-ever expedition to collect live marines for the zoo at the, then, University of Ceylon. Leading it was veteran skin-diver Vic Atukorale.

By then, we had our first swim-fins from the U.S. Army surplus. We could swim and dive a little more effectively for the elusive marines. On that trip, we brought back a fine collection of *Amphiprion clarkii*. Thirty-five beauties were collected. They lived for over a year in an unfiltered, unaerated seawater tank and were viewed by thousands of appreciative people.

Other fishes which came to the Zoo were supplied by professional anglers who used light tackle and fished them out of Colombo harbor. In those days it was a paradise for collectors— it still is, to a limited extent. One hardly could imagine that a harbor with so much shipping activity can produce such gems as *Pterois miles, Zanclus canescens, Heniochus acuminatus, Pomacanthus annularis* and *semicirculatus, Pomacentrus coelestis, Cephalopholis argus* and *boenack, Chaetodon collare, pictus, auriga, xanthocephalus* and several others, plus species of *Thalassoma, Holocentrus, Holacanthus, Labroides*, etc.

Vic Atukorale and other older professionals told me how the former Public Aquarium (closed since World War II) got its specimens from the harbor. They simply bubbled cyanide gas from the plant fumigatorium premises into the water, and up floated the fish!

Unknown to us, in the north around the magnificent rock and coral reefs, hundreds and thousands of *Chaetodon, Acanthurus* and other beauties were caught each day in wicker fish-traps for food. The real potential of this method of obtaining choice live specimens was realized only in the mid 1950's when a few full-time professionals made huge profits by buying them at cheap prices and exporting them at prices with which other countries could not compete.

Eventually, I was collecting marines regularly for the zoo aquarium. In my leisure hours I collected for one of the largest exporters of tropicals. Although my techniques were crude and my diving abilities limited, the abundance of available specimens gave me astonishing catch-averages and a fair amount of pocket money. However, it was nothing compared to what an

> They simply bubbled cyanide gas from the plant fumigatorium premises into the water and up floated the fish.

average collector earns now.

In time, the competition from other divers grew more formidable. In several years, there were at least 100 full-time professional diver-collectors in Sri Lanka. They brought in hundreds of dollars worth of fishes every day to satisfy the demands of up to 20 exporters.

The first underwater flashlight was brought to me by my former boss in the zoo, the late Major Aubrey Weinman. This opened up vast new horizons in collecting. I was able to net various species of the elusive *Zanclus, Pomacanthus* and *Chaetodon* at night with ease.

For three years I managed the tropical fish export section of a large firm. I was paid well to collect and ship. During this period, I had opportunities to travel to many new spots, including the Maldives. It was there that I collected some of the first specimens of *Pygoplites diacanthus* ever to reach public aquariums in Germany.

The first time that I used SCUBA for collecting marines, I demonstrated to the directors of my firm the efficacy of this method in the Colombo harbor. I am not quite sure as to the precise catch composition of that amazing dive off the Colombo Pilot Station, but I do remember that it was quite financially lucrative—all in less than 1 1/2 hours.

New ideas, innovations and inventions to increase efficiency and, therefore, catches, were introduced from time to time. These will be discussed and described in succeeding chapters.

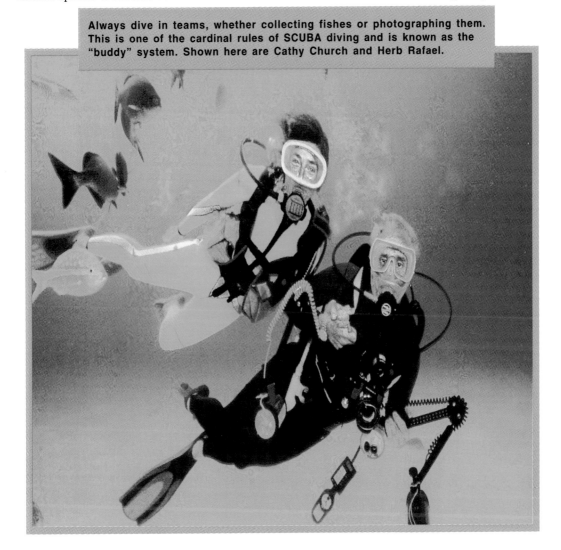

Always dive in teams, whether collecting fishes or photographing them. This is one of the cardinal rules of SCUBA diving and is known as the "buddy" system. Shown here are Cathy Church and Herb Rafael.

Choice of Location

It is obvious that one must have something of a choice of fishing spots in order to collect effectively. The depth, water temperature, visibility, nature of bottom, presence of potential discomforts and dangers, degree of pollution (if any) and various other factors need consideration.

DEPTH

The shallower the water the better it is, within reason. Spots that are too shallow are awkward to work and the specimens there (fishes, for the most part) are overly-wary or not in great abundance. Very shallow spots in more tropical waters also are too hot in the afternoon for fishes to live in. Berndt Schmidt, son of the well-known dealer in Frankfurt, Hans Schmidt, tells me that during the summertime in the Red Sea, it is virtually impossible to keep marines alive by day in aquariums or even in the shallows floating in a bait-basket. It is simply too hot!

Deeper waters have more fishes. This is particularly so in coralline locations up to about 50 feet deep. Deeper than this the corals diminish. Also, there is less variety of fishes where there is less sunlight.

Other problems arise in deep-water collecting. Fishes brought up too suddenly suffer discomfort and succumb to swim-bladder distension. They need "decompression" in slow, tedious stages. This will be dealt with in greater detail in the chapter on SCUBA diving.

The best depths for collecting tropical marine fishes are from 6 to 30 feet. Most of the desirable species are found here. On a virgin reef, you will of course find the fish more numerous and tamer than usual. In areas that have been worked over, you will have to go deeper and work harder.

Some fishes seem to "know" that they are relatively safe among the sharp venomous spines of *Diadema* sea urchins.

On pure coral reefs, the collecting is not quite as simple as it may seem. There are many escape routes and crevices, funk-holes and coral labyrinths. Nor can any fishes, except the very slow-movers like *Pterois volitans*, be pursued and netted in open water.

When free diving (holding one's breath), the best depth to work is from 12 to 24 feet. In very shallow water, it is

surprisingly difficult to work, unless you wear lead to counteract your natural buoyancy. In deeper water, unless you are an expert, your lungs and ears limit your time and energy underwater.

WATER TEMPERATURE

When the water is too warm it can keep most fish from the area. Additionally, it tends to be uncomfortable. In Colombo, April and May are the hottest months of the year. An energetic diver-collector actually sweats underwater after a few hectic minutes of chasing fish.

Cold water is also uncomfortable. Several Sri Lankan collectors wear wet-suits when the temperature drops below 75° Fahrenheit. That is considered "cold" for this part of the world!

It appears as if several marines actually are sluggish and unhappy when the water is cool. They are, in fact, easier to chase and catch at such times.

The best temperature to dive and work in is 80° Fahrenheit or thereabouts.

VISIBILITY

A diver-collector is always much happier when the water is clearest. This enables him to spot, chase and corner a desired specimen. At the same time, the fish can see much better and is correspondingly more difficult to capture. Very clear water with maximum visibility on a dark night (and the collector using a powerful flashlight) is a most effective combination for a good catch.

For the non-diver who works "blind," poor visibility in shallow conditions often yields pleasant surprises. The fish is almost as helpless in very murky water as its pursuer and captor.

Relatively murky water can be advantageous to the SCUBA diver-collector. Territorial coral fishes are reluctant to swim about. They stay close to their caves and crevices when the visibility is lessened. If the collector does not fear working in such conditions, his rewards are considerable. I often have been compelled to dive to below 30 feet in water where the maximum visibility was less than 5 feet. Choice fishes were a cinch to catch when I encountered them. Several *Balistoides conspicillum* even

have been taken by hand in such conditions, bonuses for daring to operate in rather frightening conditions.

Surprising though it may seem, some popular best-sellers are best collected in brackish estuaries and lagoons off India and Sri Lanka. Well over 50% of the thousands of young *Heniochus acuminatus* shipped from Sri Lanka come from such spots. Others such as *Chaetodon collare*, *C. pictus*, *Pterois miles*, *Promicrops lanceolatus* and even *Pomacanthus annularis* are also found in this area. Many so-called "coral fishes" are stimulated to spawn when rains or floods lower the salinity. The youngsters appear inside lagoons and estuaries and grow swiftly on the plankton-rich medium in

SCUBA gear is necessary for collecting fishes and photographing them. Limited success can be accomplished without the diving gear, but it is so much easier with it. Photo by Walter Deas.

which they live. They then swim down to the sea upon reaching the proper size or when salinity is reduced too much for their comfort. A few marines have been known to spend their entire lives within brackish water lagoons.

NATURE OF BOTTOM

This is the most important factor of all. The variety and quantity of collectable fishes depends on the nature of the bottom. On a pure sand bottom, there is virtually nothing to collect. The other extreme is a coral wilderness where there are plenty of fishes but simply too many escape routes. None of the fishes can be collected by a diver with a net, at least by day.

Marine tropicals frequent a variety of habitats, ranging from artificial reefs in the form of old car tires and junk, to virgin coral reefs, harbor walls, rocky outcrops, shipwrecks and even the proximity of larger host fishes. In spots where reefs are absent, any kind of object on the bottom becomes a sort of haven for a young marine fish (for example a *Heniochus*). In such locations, thoughtful and enterprising collectors often dump junk, tires, or old automobile bodies—anything to create a sort of oasis in an underwater

desert.

Skilled native divers in North Sri Lanka anchor huge acacia trees in depths up to 30 feet on sandy bottoms. They regularly harvest very choice food-fishes by encircling the spot with nets, removing the obstructions and then hauling the catch up into boats. In the process (and much to my regret), dozens of beauties are taken or destroyed—usually species of

Collected fishes can easily be held in nets until such time as they can be moved into holding tanks or actually packed for shipping. Photo by Rodney Jonklaas in Sri Lanka.

Pterois, Heniochus, Lutjanus and *Chaetodon.*

A natural basis of rock or coral, surrounded by an expanse of sand, is usually a gold mine for a diver-collector. Professional Sinhalese tuna fishermen know of these spots for collecting live bait. In water from 20 to 60 feet deep, they lower a large square net using two outrigger canoes for

the purpose. The center of this net is of fine mush, the perimeter much larger. After the net has settled for a few minutes and the small plankton-feeding fishes have emerged from their holes and are above it, the net is pulled up as quickly as possible by its four corners. Literally pounds of *Dascyllus, Pomacentrus, Apogon, Canthigaster, Chromis, Pseudanthias,* and a few *Chaetodon* are caught—for tuna bait!

In the Maldive Islands, Dr. Herbert Axelrod and I were astounded to find the catch composition from one bait-boat to be 75% young *Chaetodon kleinii.* Cedric Martenstyn, my one-time star diver-collector, had spend more than half an hour chasing and netting one the morning before!

The success of Sri Lankan diver-collectors is attributable to the very productive bottom they work in. The finest bottom is one that is composed of smooth gneiss or granite rock on which corals grow. Here one encounters both the genuine coral-haunting species as well as others like *Chaetodon pictus, Heniochus acuminatus* and *Pterois miles.* A rocky bottom is much easier to work than a coral one, especially by day.

If you are angling with light tackle for marines (and this is the best and only way to get several of them, particularly the wrasses), any kind of bottom, as long as there are fishes over it, will do. More about angling in a succeeding chapter.

A harbor with fairly clear water is a superb spot for collecting. Even on the surface, young *Platax* can be netted from off a boat or off the wall itself, with a long-handled net. The man-made corners and walls, overgrown with clams, sea-fans and barnacles, are beloved by marines of many species. Colombo harbor is a regular treasure-trove. And even though it has been exploited by diver-collectors for over 20 years, it still does not disappoint those who explore its depths.

A ship-wreck harbors a whole lot of fish, but hunting in or around it requires care. The rusty parts can cause troublesome abrasions and ruin a net which is inexpertly wielded.

Eelgrass bottoms have a surprisingly rich fauna. A small seine-net worked "blind" or with divers can provide several wrasses, sea horses, young *Chaetodon* and snappers.

A bottom almost paved with giant anemones, of course, is marvelous for big hauls of *Amphiprion* and *Dascyllus trimaculatus*.

DISCOMFORTS AND DANGERS

I need hardly mention that diving and collecting on a coral reef has its attendant minor problems—which on and off may assume major proportions. If I am asked what I consider to be the most important item for a collector (apart from a net), I would unhesitatingly say "gloves". They are essential, unless you have extra-tough hands and fingers and do not mind cuts, bites, stings, lacerations and bruises!

Although it is more comfortable and faster to wear only swimtrunks on a tropical marine collecting trip, other articles of wear and gadgetry become necessary depending on the nature of terrain, weather conditions, etc. There will be a detailed discussion of gear and apparel in a chapter devoted to this.

Many corals and gorgonians sting. So do crown-of-thorns starfish, mostly every jellyfish, all anemones and most sea urchins.

Many crabs bite. Most morays like to experiment with their jaws on unusual, tantalizing objects, like human fingers. A triggerfish gives a nasty bite. *Pterois*, as you know, has a very poisonous sting. There are several books on dangerous marine organisms. It is well to read them before you try to become anything of a collector.

Do not preclude the danger of sunburn, especially if you are a tidepool and fossicking type, like many on the Great Barrier Reef. Wear a hat, of course. Only the hardiest souls would dare walk on dead or living coral without ankle-high sneakers or rope-soles.

Underwater, jellyfish can be more than a nuisance at times. Although the average alert skin-diver can avoid the larger medusae, it is the thousands of smaller one in planktonic concentrations that can keep you out of the water. Wearing a wet-suit complete with hood helps—you get stung only on the face and lips! A cotton balletsuit, or leotards and turtle-neck jacket is the next best thing.

Very rough seas are always

Dr. Herbert R. Axelrod has spent many hours below the surface collecting and photographing fishes. Here he is homing in on a subject at Marau, Solomon Islands.

hazardous. Even underwater with SCUBA, a collector can get knocked against corals and sharp rocks.

The ultimate in underwater danger, sharks and other potentially aggressive fishes are very real problems when one is

Avoid Polluted waters for your own sake!

operating in the more remote spots like the Maldives. I need hardly add that the buddy-system should be more or less compulsory in places like this. As a matter of fact, having a buddy underwater, or any place else, makes a tremendous difference to your frame of mind—and to your catch.

One must not forget man-made dangers. Careless outboarders are one of the worst. Also, a thoughtless coxswain can fling an anchor right on top of you when you are underwater. And, as has happened before, a lazy tender can doze off and not wake up to spot you calling to be picked up well away from your boat.

Common sense and a fair amount of book-knowledge should combine to provide you with the safety margin that is so essential to collecting. Experience comes with time, but it is wiser to ensure that it comes over a relatively long period of time.

In short, steer well away from any place which may be dangerous or uncomfortable, particularly if there is an alternative spot.

POLLUTION

Although the area in which you wish to collect may appear clear, calm and safe, it may be polluted. I was once severely stricken with allergic bumps all over my body having collected in a rather sheltered part of Colombo harbor. The place was teeming with fish—mainly the supposedly delicate Moorish Idols (*Zanclus canescens*). I found out later that a barge laden with grain had sunk there. The fermentation had not been dispersed due to the sheltered water.

It is astonishing how much pollution fish can stand! Schools of surgeon-fishes and pomacentrids are quite happy in effluvia from public lavatories. The outlet of a treatment plant off Colombo regularly yields *Heniochus*, *Pterois* and even a *Pomacanthus semicirculatus* or two!

Avoid polluted waters, for your own sake.

TIME AND TIDES

They say "time and tide wait for no man," but man certainly can wait for them, especially when he wants to collect those rare marines.

With experience, you will find out what the best times are to go for certain fishes. Nighttime, of course, is best for catching surgeons, butterflyfishes and squirrelfishes, but you will not succeed with the wrasses, pomacentrids and

clownfishes after dark.

In the Maldives, I discovered that the *Pseudanthias squamipinnis* were almost impossible to catch by day with SCUBA gear using any kind of a net. But quite by chance, I found out that just before it gets dark in the evening they tend to hover around their intended sleeping-holes and can be netted very efficiently over these spots.

In lagoons and estuaries it is only common sense to wait for the clear water of the high tide to improve visibility. The height of the tide is of course the best time, but of very short duration. Tropical tides are not high and the flow is not always so strong as to keep an average diver out of the water.

Off Singapore, the tides are higher than off Sri Lanka. Most of the diver-collectors there wait for low tide when clownfish and anemones can be netted in water less than 4 ft. deep!

Light tackle angling for wrasses is best done at the turn of the tide. They are eager and hungry, and take almost any bait. In the evening, they are about to rest for the night and are interested only mildly in food.

Young morays seem to like hunting about in shallow water, rushing over a reef with the incoming tide. At other times, they are seldom seen from the surface.

Keep careful notes of your observations and refer to them later on to help you find the best time and spot to get the best collection. It pays.

The Complete Marine Collectors Gear

In the next few chapters I will be referring to various items of gear associated with collecting. Rather than deviate by describing them individually, I will list them here in a rough form of classification. The truly "complete" collector could have a collection of gear costing up to thousands of dollars—the professionals certainly do. As this book is intended for both amateurs and professionals, a reasonably comprehensive list is given with plenty of room for improvements and expansion.

1. *Books, maps, charts and guides:* These are indispensable to the serious collector, and their choice depends on what is required and where one intends to operate.

2. *Apparel:* Tough but airy clothes, hats, sneakers, socks, gloves, swim-trunks and wet suits or similar protective clothing.

3. *Viewing aids:* Binoculars, dive-masks, magnifying glasses, glass-bottomed bucket for non-swimmers.

4. *Swimming aids:* Swimfins or flippers. For the top pros in the Cousteau class, underwater scooters.

5. *Transportation:* Suitable land vehicles, boats, trailers and, of course, the available regular transportation services.

6. *Collecting apparatus:*

Nets of various sizes, probes, squeeze-bottles for use of soporifics, traps, light rods and tackle, slurp-guns, spearguns.

7. *Illumination:* Flashlights or rechargeable lights for underwater and surface use.

Underwater Rodney Jonklaas "bags" his catch, an anemonefish, carefully

Lanterns for emergency.

8. *Live fish storage:* Cans, plastic containers, plastic bags, rubber bands, oxygen, live bait wells, live-fish floating containers, aquariums, aerators or compressed-air cylinders.

9. *Specialized diving-gear:* Self-contained Underwater Breathing Apparatus (SCUBA) with portable air supply, compressor or large air-storage cylinders.

10. *Safety gear:* Life-jackets, inflatable life-jackets, knives, safety reel and line, flares, whistles, etc.

11. *First-aid:* A box with specialized drugs and dressings as scissors, hypodermic syringe and anti-venom for serious stings, ammonia for minor stings, antiseptic, seasickness pills, band-aids, small suturing needle and catgut.

12. *Fish medicaments:* Antibiotics, tranquilizers, fine needle, scissors.

13. *Recording gear:* Cameras (preferably underwater type like the Nikonos, which also can be used on the surface), sketchbook, notebook, indelible ink.

14. *Fish preserving gear:* Formalin, containers for preserved fish, labels, label pen.

15. *Miscellaneous:* An all-around, all-purpose tool kit for maintenance and repairs for all gear, mechanical and electrical.

This list may look formidable and no doubt it is, but it is useful for reference. No expedition of a serious nature to collect marines can be successful without reference to every aspect.

Behavior of Tropical Marine Fishes

It is useful, if not necessary, to know something of the habits of tropical marines before you try to collect them. That is, if you want to do it with some success and economy. If you have all the time in the world to spare—in which case you are an extremely fortunate person—it is fun to find out for yourself.

Family by family, let's briefly discuss the habits and mannerisms of the tropicals that can be collected, and the problems that confront you in respect to those that cannot!

(1) SMALL SHARKS AND RAYS

The semi-sedentary nurse-sharks (*Ginglymostoma sp.*)

Blacktip Shark (*Carcharhinus melanopterus*). Photo by Ken Lucas.

lurk in rocks and caves. They can be caught easily by (gloved) hand by day or night. Predatory sharks like the blacktip (*Carcharinus melanoptera*), which in its

Round Stingray (*Urolophus halleri*) female. Photo by Scott Michael.

smaller sizes of less than 2 feet makes an ideal pet for an ambitious marine enthusiast, can be trapped only in a tide-pool by several collectors, or taken on a baited hook.

Small rays and skates are quite easy to net by night. Even by day the electric rays (*Narcine timlei*) are slow and easily netted. Be prepared for a shock, though, if you use a metal net frame and handle which conduct electricity. Electric rays frequent sand, coral and rocky bottoms, from 6 to 60 feet deep.

(2) LIZARDFISHES

Young lizardfish (*Synodus* sp.). Photo by Roger Steene.

(SYNODONTIDAE)

These bizarre but intricately marked fellows are common reef dwellers,

preferring to lie on elevated coral heads over sandy bottoms. They make sudden darts at their prey. They are easiest to collect with a baited hook. Netting them is easy with two divers—one with a big net, the other driving the fish into it.

(3) CATFISH (PLOTOSIDAE)

Plotosus lineatus is a collector's dream. It can be found by day in caves and

Stinging Catfish (*Plotosus lineatus*).

crevices. It can be netted literally by the dozen, with ease. Smaller ones sometimes gather in moving balls and swim in the open. They are even easier to collect.

Green Moray Eel (*Gymnothorax funebris*) cleaned by young *Bodianus*. Photo by Dr. W. A. Starck II.

(4) MORAYS (MURAENIDAE)

Morays are not easy to collect. One species, *M. nebulosa*, is common. It can be netted on shallow reefs at the turn of the tide. Others, like *M. tesselata*, are shy and exhausting to pry out of their holes into a net. The best method is to use a powerful soporific tranquilizer. Larger morays take baited hooks, but extracting the hook from the jaws is difficult and tricky. Some species entwine themselves in branched coral heads. They can be lifted out complete with coral and shaken into a bucket. They bite, so mind your fingers!

(5) SNAKE-EELS

Baja Snake Eel (*Ophichthus erabo*). Photo by Dr. R. E. Thresher.

(OPHICHTHYIDAE)

These beautiful and inoffensive creatures swim slowly and confidently in and out of corals and rocks in the shallows. They are very easy to corner and net, even by someone who is wading.

Species which burrow

Asian Trumpetfish (*Aulostomus chinensis*). Photo by Alex Kerstitch.

require strong tranquilizers to knock them out and so make their capture easy.

(6) FLUTEMOUTHS (AULOSTOMIDAE)

These fish swim in mid-water and have good eyesight.

Bluespotted Cornetfish (*Fistularia tabacaria*). Photo by Charles Arneson.

Netting them by day is difficult. Go after them by night. Use a net with a very long bag.

(7) CORNETFISHES (FISTULARIDAE)

The same technique as for the flutemouths works with these. Care should be taken not to injure their long and semi-rigid bodies.

(8) PIPEFISHES AND SEA HORSES (SYNGNATHIDAE)

These are among the

Bay Pipefish (*Syngnathus leptorhynchus*). Photo by Ken Lucas, Steinhart Aquarium.

easiest of marines to net, once spotted, even by an absolute novice. The pipefishes like crawling or swimming about among the corals.

If you can spot a sea horse, catching him, even with your

Longsnout Sea Horse (*Hippocampus reidi*). Photo by Cathy Church, Grand Cayman.

fingers, is a cinch. Most species live in eel-grass beds. They can be collected simply by sweeping a big net through the fronds.

(9) SQUIRRELFISHES (HOLOCENTRIDAE)

These nocturnal fishes are netted easily at night by divers using powerful flashlights. Their spines render them speedily enmeshed in most nets and they seldom get away. A light-tackle angler can catch dozens at night on shallow reefs. By day it is possible for one or two divers with long-handled nets to fish them out of deep caves and crevices in which they congregate.

Crown Squirrelfish (*Sargocentron diadema*). Photo by John O'Malley.

Striped Mullet (*Mugil cephalus*). Photo by Dr. Fujio Yasuda.

(10) GRAY MULLET (MUGILIDAE)

One species from India and Sri Lanka, *Mugil vaigiensis*, is attractively marked with yellow fins. It makes a fine pet. It swims rather swiftly near the surface in estuaries and river-mouths. It can be netted by two collectors using a big seine. By night it

Glass Perchlet (*Ambassis macracantha*). Photo by Noel Gray.

is easier. A long-handled net can do the job.

(11) GLASSFISH (CENTROPOMIDAE)

A few marine glassfish are attractive. They are about the easiest of fishes to collect by diving. The diver simply swims up to masses of them poised before coral and rock caves and sweeps dozens into this net!

(12) GROUPERS (SERRANIDAE)

Groupers essentially are

cave-dwellers. They are not easy to collect. Although most groupers take a baited hook, their swim-bladders do not take kindly to being

Honeycomb Grouper (*Epinephelus merra*). Photo by Glen S. Axelrod.

de-pressurized from deep water to land or a boat. Diver-collectors who work in pairs get better results than individually. By night, if you can find a grouper, he is easy to catch. Most specimens have to be "tickled" out of their caves with a probe or piece of wire and then chased into a waiting net with a big bag.

Coral Rockcod (*Cephalopholis miniata*). Photo by Gunter Spies.

Promicrops lanceolatus, in its gorgeous gold and black juvenile stages, usually comes from traps set in brackish lagoons by professional fishermen. The rare blue grouper (*Epinephelus flavocoeruleus*) is, fortunately, very prone to

jamming itself in a hole or piece of coral and so is easier to collect than most. The very choice *Cephalopholis miniatus* lives in deep coral caves. It is very difficult to collect. It also is difficult to bring up to the surface because of swim bladder problems. The smaller the specimen, the easier to de-pressurize it.

Two-banded Grouper (*Diploprion bifasciatum*). Photo by Dr. Warren E. Burgess.

(13) SEA-PERCHES (DIPLOPRIONIDAE)

Diploprion bifasciatum is common off Sri Lanka, India, and Malaysia. It is less difficult to corner than most groupers. At night it is firmly wedged in coral and easily persuaded to dart into a net. Remember that *Diploprion* exudes a deadly poison when alarmed, so to put it with other fishes is disastrous. In a poorly ventilated container it will even poison itself to death!

(14) TARGET-PERCH (TERAPONIDAE)

Baby terapons shoal in brackish river-mouths in very shallow water. Collectors wading with nets can net them easily. Bigger specimens gobble any kind of bait with zest and are easily taken.

Target-Perch (*Terapon jarbua*).
Photo by Andre Roth.

(15) FLAGTAILS (KUHLIIDAE)
Kuhlia taeniura is very
much a tide-pool fish which

Barred Flagtail (*Kuhlia taeniura*).
Photo by Dr. Herbert R. Axelrod.

also likes turbulent, surfy
conditions. A wader, or even a
non-swimmer with a mask
and net, can chase them in
tide-pools and collect them
quite easily. Bigger specimens
strike at a moving bait close to
the surface.

Japanese Bigeye (*Pristigenys
niphonia*). Photo by G. W.
Lange.

(16) BIGEYES (PRIACANTHIDAE)
These big-eyed red fish are
nocturnal and can be netted
by night in the same manner
as the squirrelfishes.

(17) CARDINALFISHES (APOGONIDAE)
Shoals of cardinals all but
block the entrances of coral
caves and are so easily netted
as to be a nuisance to
collectors seeking more
elusive fishes in the same

Whitestar Cardinalfish (*Apogon
lachneri*). Photo by Courtney
Platt.

territory. They are nocturnal
and cannot see very well by
day. As a result, they always
fall victim to a net being
swished in their direction.
This is one reason why they
are so inexpensive.

(18) JACKS (CARANGIDAE)
Very small jacks can be
netted from off a boat or in the
shallows by a wader, but if
they are longer than 1 inch,
they become more difficult to
catch. Immature golden jacks
(*Gnathanodon speciosus*), the
most desirable of them all,
behave like pilot-fish
(*Naucrates*) in their juvenile
stages following big fish and
skin-divers around. If you see
a black and gold striped
beauty swimming in front of
your nose, swish a net there

Golden Jack (*Gnathanodon
speciosus*). Photo by U. E.
Friese.

and you have a baby golden
jack. Bigger ones congregate
round larger groupers,
sharks, turtles—even puffers.
Often, if you spear a big
grouper, you collect a bonus
of baby jacks which refuse to
leave their host. This is why I
have included a speargun in
my list of gear for collecting.
Pelagic jacks readily hit a
lure and with light tackle you
can collect some nice-sized
specimens which are hardy
and will grow fast, too fast, in
an aquarium.

(19) SNAPPERS (LUTJANIDAE)
The smaller snappers, or
juveniles of big species, are
desirable for aquariums and,
fortunately, easy to collect.

Emperor Snapper (*Lutjanus
sebae*). Photo by John O'Malley.

Very small *Lutjanus kasmira*
shoal by the hundreds in
water about 20-30 feet deep
over coral and rock reefs. They
can be netted easily by a

SCUBA diver. Larger ones greedily take bait and can be hooked by the dozen. The spectacular *Lutjanus sebae* lives around poisonous sea urchins, *Diadema*, and will not swim away into the open. So even holding one's breath, an average diver-collector can catch them. Bigger specimens enter fish-traps whence they reach collectors.

Two-lined Monocle Bream (*Scolopsis bilineatus*). Photo by Dr. W. A. Starck II.

(20) SCOLOPSIDS (SCOLOPSIDAE)

There is at least one attractive species, *Scolopsis ghanam*, which will take a bait offered it by a wading angler. In its smaller stages, it can be chased in among coral and rocks and collected by net.

(21) SWEETLIPS

Goldmann's Sweetlips (*Plectorhinchus goldmanni*). Photo by Dr. John E. Randall.

(PLECTORHYNCHIDAE)

Very small sweetlips, like the juveniles of *Plectorhinchus lineatusm* and *pictus*, are brightly colored, wriggly and terrified of moving away from their territory. This is usually an outcrop of rock, coral or wreckage over a sandy bottom. So netting them is easy. When they get larger, they are more venturesome, and correspondingly harder to catch.

Sweetlips feed by night. They can see well by day and by night. Using a very brilliant underwater flashlight helps while night-diving.

Plectorhinchus chaetodonoides from Singapore, Indonesia and Malaysia is a nippy fish, very difficult to chase and collect in coral reefs, as I found to my cost in Singapore.

Larger specimens enter traps and are taken alive by professional fishermen. Fortunately, there are definite breeding seasons for sweetlips. When there are young about, there are plenty of them.

Many Banded Goatfish (*Parupeneus multifasciatus*). Photo by Dr. Gerald R. Allen.

(22) GOATFISHES (MULLIDAE)

A few species are brightly colored enough to be desirable to collectors. By night, when they turn red and sleep on the sand-bottom in the open or around rocks and corals, they are very easy to collect indeed.

(23) BATFISHES (PLATACIDAE)

Baby batfish drift like dead leaves on the surface and even a kid of five can catch them from a boat or jetty with a long-handled net. When they

Platax pinnatus is the most colorful of the batfishes. Photo by Earl Kennedy.

get bigger, they get "smarter" and a diver must go after them. They like to frequent sheltered inlets and coves, usually where dead leaves float. Corners of tropical harbors are favorite spots during the season for babies.

(24) ANGELFISHES (POMACANTHIDAE)

The prime targets of collectors, professional and amateur, many species of angelfish are perhaps the most sought-after of marine tropicals. They are essentially coral and rock dwellers and are never found in open water. They are also fiercely territorial. This is their undoing, because if you fail to net one by day, go to the same spot by night with a powerful flashlight and its yours.

Apolemichthys xanthurus and *Centropyge* species like to

Emperor Angelfish (*Pomacanthus imperator*). Photo by John O'Malley.

wedge themselves in coral or rocks at night. They are not readily netted. By day, however, they are fairly easy to corner, although coral angelfish are extremely difficult to catch. One must choose suitable spots and not waste time trying to catch one where it has every advantage with its multitude of hiding places.

Small juveniles of all angelfishes are much easier to

Flame Angelfish (*Centropyge loriculus*). Photo by John O'Malley.

collect than the medium-sized ones which are the most sought after. The adults, too, are easy. The escape-holes are often too small for them. In panic, they wedge themselves in and can be pulled out carefully by hand.

Many of the angelfishes fall foul of traps. In Singapore, hundreds of *Chaetodontoplus*

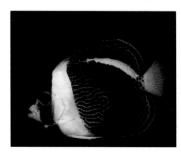

Duboulay's Angelfish (*Chaetodontoplus duboulayi*). Photo by Dr. Herbert R. Axelrod.

mesoleucus are obtained in this fashion. Divers have much less luck trying to corner them by day or by night in the shallow and not-too-clear coral jungles around this island.

(25) BUTTERFLYFISHES (CHAETODONTIDAE)

Most butterflyfishes are almost as territorially-minded as the angelfishes, but do not hole-up as readily. Some species like to shoal as adults (*Heniochus acuminatus*, *Chaetodon collare*) while others remain in pairs (*Chaetodon xanthocephalus*, *Heniochus singularius*).

Others seem to live only in deep water (*Chaetodon*

Red-tailed Butterflyfish (*Chaetodon collare*). Photo by John O'Malley.

chrysurus). A few love the shallows, less than 20 feet deep (*Chaetodon octofasciatus*).

Butterflyfishes have varied territorial preferences and it is important for the prospective collector to study these. Coral-feeders like *Chaetodon plebeius* or *trifasciatus* may stray away from coral during day, but will always rest at night in between the fronds or under the branches.

Nearly all chaetodontids

Bannerfish (*Heniochus acuminatus*). Photo by John O'Malley.

change color by night. They get darker markings and are often difficult to identify.

The smaller the butterflyfish is, the easier it is to collect. But here again, it is the medium to average-sized specimens that are the most sought-after and best suited to aquarium life.

In a few species the adults will often dash into caves when panicked by one or more divers (*Chaetodon xanthocephalus*). Others seem to go on forever and tire out the diver rather than get tired themselves.

Generally, the best way to collect butterflyfishes is at night, after having studied them in the evening and watched their movements before they choose their

Long-nosed Butterflyfish (*Forcipiger flavissimus*). Photo by Dr. Herbert R. Axelrod.

resting-spots. A careful observer will note that *Forcipiger flavissimus* sneaks under mushroom shaped corals, turns neutral gray in color and suspends itself upside-down from the roof of its cave!

Forcipiger juveniles are very easy to collect when chased by day. The adults are a little nippier, but can be cornered. Once they raise their dorsals and hesitate, they can be yours if you are a fair SCUBA diver.

Chaetodon species enter traps, and paradoxically those which steadfastly refuse food in aquaria are the most commonly found in fish-traps in northeastern Sri Lanka (*Chaetodon trifasciatus*). A few even take bait on very light tackle (*Heniochus acuminatus*) and all will fall foul of soporifics, of course.

A group of divers can chase adult butterflyfishes into a set-net on shallow coral reefs, but the mortality from

Eight-striped Butterflyfish (*Chaetodon octofasciatus*). Photo by K. H. Choo.

damaged and de-scaled specimens after this type of capture is considerable. Prolonged chasing of adults in sharp staghorn corals results in considerable bruising and scale. Most of the catch subsequently succumbs to infected abrasions.

At least one species in its juvenile form (*Chaetodon octofasciatus*) is so numerous

in corals that the old favorite method of collecting *Dascyllus aruanus*, that of breaking off such a coral and shaking it over a bucket, effectively can be adopted here. However, I am much against the breaking and destruction of corals anywhere. I favor the night-diving method for collecting butterflyfishes or any other coral-haunting fishes for that matter.

Skunk-striped Anemonefish (*Amphiprion akallopisos*). Photo by M. P. & C. Piednoir.

(26) DAMSELFISHES AND CLOWNFISHES (POMACENTRIDAE)

These are essentially territorial fishes, perhaps even the most so of all tropical marines. With a little perseverance, any pomacentrid is yours to be collected. Clownfishes will never leave anemones, although in a garden of *Radianthus* a clever clown will flit from one to another and lead you a merry chase.

Amphiprion nigripes is one of the nippiest of the clowns. It often leaves its anemones and hides under corals or rocks.

Amphiprion sebae prefers sand-anemones. Adults literally enter their host anemones and disappear with them as they slowly contract.

Yellow-bellied Blue Damsel (*Pomacentrus caeruleus*). Photo by Dr. John E. Randall.

With a gloved hand thrust into the "mouth" of the anemone, one can fairly easily seize the fish and pull it out.

Some pomacentrids (*Pomacentrus coelestis*) swarm and shoal over small corals, rocks and sand. They can be "herded" by one or two divers using a big net. This way up to 20 specimens can be netted in just one breath.

Others, like *Dascyllus carneus* and *D. aruanus*, live only around corals into which they rush when alarmed. So break off the coral head, shake it into a bucket of

Marginate Damselfish (*Dascyllus marginatus*). Photo by Dr. Gerald R. Allen.

water, and then take it back and place it carefully in the same spot where it will continue growing.

Adult *Dascyllus trimaculatus* get large and

hungry enough to take small baited hooks, as do sergeant majors (*Abudefduf saxatilis*), but the latter enter fish-traps in Sri Lanka by the hundreds. There seems to be no better way of getting them in adult sizes.

Most pomacentrids live in shallow water, but some clownfishes occur deeper than 60 feet as long as there are anemones for them to seek shelter in.

(27) WRASSES (LABRIDAE)

Whereas most wrasses are fast-moving and difficult to net, one or two, like juvenile *Coris*, swim close to the bottom and hole-up quickly so that a diver with a net can take them easily.

Adult wrasses are very lovely. A clever diver or wading angler with ultra-light tackle can fish selectively for those he desires. They eagerly

Cortez Rainbow Wrasse (*Thalassoma lucasanum*). Photo by Courtney Platt.

bite on shrimp, clam or octopus bait. Every species shows a variation in mode of feeding. A *Thalassoma hardwicki* literally will dash at a white speck in mid-water (which is your bait), whereas a *Bodianus diana* or *Halichoeres hortulanus* prefers to inspect it on the bottom first and then engulf it. Adult *Thalassoma lunare* enter traps, as do the magnificent male *Gomphosus varius*. *Thalassoma*

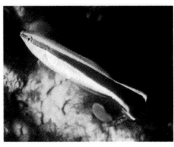

Bluestreak Cleaner Wrasse (*Labroides dimidiatus*).

purpureum, which likes active, almost foamy shallow water to feed in, will take a hook only in such locations.

By night, wrasses are very difficult to spot. They sleep quite deep in corals and entwined in their fronds, seemingly immune from predatory morays, crabs and the like.

Young wrasses can be netted with big fine-meshed nets. The majority of the cleaner-wrasses (*Labroides dimidiatus*) are obtained in this fashion. But a SCUBA diver often is approached by these enterprising creatures for a clean-up. He systematically can net these fine, big adults, if he has a big net and is agile enough.

Queen Parrotfish (*Scarus vetula*). Photo by Courtney Platt.

(28) PARROTFISHES (SCARIDAE)

Few collectors go in for parrotfishes since they are usually too large for the average aquarium. The only way to get them is by night, netting them in their sleep. Traps yield specimens, but

they are almost always too large. Netting them by day even with SCUBA is a waste of time and energy.

(29) BLENNIES (BLENNIIDAE)

It all depends on what the blenny you are looking for feeds on. If it is an *Aspidontus*, it will try to feed off you! So a diver with a net has no difficulty in netting these saber-tooths. As a matter of fact, a good many suppliers of fish to Sri Lankan

False Cleanerfish (*Aspidontus taeniatus*). Photo by Dr. Herbert R. Axelrod.

exporters mix up saber-toothed blennies with *Labroides dimidiatus*, which they closely resemble.

Most blennies are small and easy to collect. Using a metal probe, one can persuade a holed-up blenny to rush out into a waiting net, even in tide-pools.

Axelrod's Blenny (*Ecsenius axelrodi*). Photo by Dr. John E. Randall.

Blennies favor coral and rock reefs and tide-pools. Only the most colorful are sought-after. There are not too many of them.

Foxface (*Lo vulpinus*).

(30) RABBITFISHES (SIGANIDAE)

Only the juveniles of these largish food-fishes are attractive, and then not very much so, except the spectacular *Lo vulpinus* from Malaysia, Indonesia and the Philippines. Since they are algae and weed eaters, they readily fall foul of baited fish-traps and no doubt a major part of the world's supply comes from these sources.

Night-divers find siganids easy to collect. They rest motionless in shallow water, literally leaning against rocks or corals with fins erect. They seem to be easily blinded by the glare of an average flashlight.

(31) MOORISH IDOLS (ZANCLIDAE)

The spectacular Moorish Idol is almost impossible to get by day. But by night, with

Moorish Idol (*Zanclus canescens*). Photo by John O'Malley.

colors faded, they are about the easiest fishes for a diver to catch. Idols enter fish-traps with algae readily, and hundreds are obtained in North Sri Lanka this way.

(32) SURGEONFISHES, UNICORNFISHES AND TANGS (ACANTHURIDAE)

Only the very small specimens of this family, up to 2 inches, can be caught easily and economically during the day by divers. Waders in rock pools can, with some luck and using a mask or glass-bottomed box, net juvenile

Powder-blue Tang (*Acanthurus leucosternon*). Photo by Ken Lucas, Steinhart Aquarium.

Acanthurus triostegus.

Tangs or surgeons and unicornfishes essentially are reef-lovers. They have some territorial instinct. This enables one to watch where they hover in the evening and go diving for them at night with a flashlight.

Naso unicornis jams itself into rocks with spines erect like the siganids. The same is true of *Naso lituratus* and *brevirostris. Acanthurus leucosternon* likes to rest among the corals, but in well-collected areas it hides in caves and is caught with difficulty. *Paracanthurus hepatus*, probably the most spectacular of them all, is also

Orange-spine Unicornfish (*Naso lituratus*). Photo by Klaus Paysan.

the easiest to catch. It jams itself into the branches of coral when alarmed. All you have to do is to bring up the coral and shake its contents into a bucket. *Zebrasoma* species like branched corals to rest in. They are more difficult to spot and catch than most tangs.

(33) GOBIES (GOBIIDAE)

Not all gobies are lovely. The few brightly-colored ones are best caught by pairs of divers or waders, using masks or glass-bottomed buckets. One holds a big, deep net over the hole a goby has entered and the other prods it out with a slender metal rod.

Gobies which live in the open are easier to collect. When they are small, they do not seem to be overly-nervous of a big net placed close to them. The neon goby of the

Firefish (*Nemateleotris magnifica*). Photo by Dr. Walter A. Starck II.

Caribbean is said to be collected with a slurp-gun. However, my experiences with slurp-guns are far from successful. If you can place something close enough to a fish to slurp it in, you may as well use a net and net it. So why encumber yourself with underwater artillery?

(34) LIONFISHES, AND SCORPIONFISHES (SCORPAENIDAE)

These are about the easiest of the spectacular marines to collect. Juvenile *Pterois volitans* are so "confident" of their spines' stinging power that they just raise them when a

Spotfin Lionfish (*Pterois antennata*). Photo by John O'Malley.

net is placed over them. Hundreds turn up in shallows waters, especially in river and lagoon mouth, during the breeding season.

Pterois antennata occurs around soft corals in deeper water of up to 70 feet. It is more nocturnally inclined than *miles*. *Pterois radiata*, the best of them all, is purely nocturnal and rarely seen, let alone collected, by day. Look for them in coral reefs under ledges. *Dendrochirus* likes deep water, too. It is inconspicuous as it nestles close to weed and algae-covered corals or rocks.

An escaped *Pterois miles* often becomes very wary. It rushes into caves with its fins

Shortfin Lionfish (*Dendrochirus brachypterus*). Photo by John O'Malley.

folded, not to reappear until hours later. Save time by probing for him. If you tie an octopus tentacle at the end of your probe and wiggle it about, he will rush out. Lionfish hate octopuses!

(35) TRIGGERFISHES (BALISTIDAE)

Triggerfishes are among the few marines that can actually be caught by hand more effectively and surely than by any other method. Diving for them, of course, is necessary. Triggers specialize in jamming themselves in coral, rocks or wreckage when alarmed. So, basically, all one needs to do is to alarm them.

Rhinecanthus aculeatus lives in very shallow, coralline spots. It can be collected even by a

Clown Triggerfish (*Balistoides conspicillum*). Photo by Dr. Herbert R. Axelrod.

wader using a mask. In contrast, *Odonus niger* prefers depths like the celebrated

Balistoides conspicillum and the even rarer *Pseudobalistes fuscus*.

Often it is necessary to break the rock or coral to get at the trigger. A handy, all-purpose hammer is useful for a diver to carry about.

Redtooth Triggerfish (*Odonus niger*). Photo by John O'Malley.

Odonus niger seems to choose the narrowest, most tortuous crevices to hide in. The use of a squeeze-bottle of soporific drug or MS 222 helps put them to sleep, relaxing them, after which it is simple to stuff them in a container where they soon recover.

(36) FILEFISHES (MONACANTHIDAE)

These fishes do not hole up so readily and willingly as triggerfishes. They are, nevertheless, rather slow underwater and can be chased, cornered and netted by an average SCUBA diver. *Alutera scripta* often turns up in its juvenile stages drifting with seaweed or debris in mid-water. Fishermen in boats simply scoop them up with hand-nets off West Sri Lanka in April.

Scribbled Filefish (*Aluterus scriptus*). Photo by Alex Kerstitch.

Polka Dot Boxfish (*Ostracion cubicus*). Photo by Dr. Gerald R. Allen.

(37) BOXFISHES AND COWFISHES (OSTRACIONTIDAE)

Boxfishes haunt reefs and rocks in both surfy and sheltered waters. Although they are not given to jamming themselves into crevices, they are pretty adept at dodging about in them. The smaller the boxfish, the easier it is to collect. Very small *Ostracion cubicus* are cute and seem to be confused when confronted with a net under ledges. They often swim into it trustingly. The adult *Ostracion meleagris* are often encountered in shallow, surfy waters and are elusive.

By night, boxfish rest in or

Smooth Trunkfish (*Lactophrys triqueter*). Photo by Courtney Platt.

by caves. They are collected with ease, even by hand. Cowfish (*Lactoria cornuta*) seldom are seen by day. They prefer sand-bottomed marine lagoons where they hover around isolated outcrops of coral or rock. The cofferfish (*Tetrasomus gibbosus*) is of similar habit. But if you know where to find them by night, you can get a good haul. Use SCUBA gear and look around patches of coral growing on sand bottom from 30 to 60 feet deep. They will be hovering around these outcrops in search of food. Netting them is all too simple.

Remember that boxfish, the cowfish and the cofferfish all exude poison in varying degrees of toxicity and volume. No other fishes can be stored, even temporarily, in the same container with them.

Balloonfish (*Diodon holacanthus*). Photo by Ken Lucas, Steinhart Aquarium.

(38) PORCUPINEFISHES (DIODONTIDAE)

Diodon spcies breed annually or once in two years. At times the young are found by the hundreds, mostly by night, in the same kind of locations as the coffers. They are slow and easily netted. *Diodon holacanthus* hides under small rocks or corals by day. It is netted easily by raising the rock and swishing the net underneath.

(39) CANTHIGASTERS (CANTHIGASTERIDAE)

These popular miniature puffers are collected easily by divers. The young often enter lagoons and are not really fast

Spotted Sharpnose Puffer (*Canthigaster punctatissimus*). Photo by Courtney Platt.

enough to elude a big net held by a diver. *Canthigaster margaritatus* is the most common. The adults, in pairs, can be found in depths varying from 10 to 70 feet over coral or rock bottom. *Canthigaster valentini* is more of a coral lover. It is less numerous, lives deeper, and is correspondingly more elusive.

Orange-banded Blowfish (*Torquigener hypselogeneion*). Photo by Dr. Gerald R. Allen.

(40) PUFFERS (TETRAODONTIDAE)

Baby puffers swim close to the surface. They are easy to net even from a boat. The bigger puffers have the same habits as diodons. They can be seen at night by SCUBA divers over sand and coral bottoms.

I have described only very briefly the general habits and mannerisms of the more popularly-collected tropical marines. There are many variations and deviations. Even individuals of the same species sometime behave unusually.

Above: The crystal clear water of El Nido, Palawan, Philippines, teems with fishes, apparently not at all concerned about sharing their home with a human. Photo by Guy van den Bossche.

Below: Divers often find that the local fishes are very friendly in areas where they are not hunted and will sometimes allow themselves even to be touched. Photo by Herb Rafael.

There is no better way to prepare to collect marines than to watch them carefully at all times of the day and, if possible, by night. Then plan your campaign. Too often I have met visiting enthusiasts armed with pet store nets, shiny aerators, plastic buckets and a dozen gadgets which fail under real conditions. After ruining much of their gear and with aching and sunburned bodies, they get the hang of the collecting game in a few days, after which it is time to fly back to Europe or America!

I hope this book will cut down on some of these frustrations and bitter experiences.

Keeping Your Fishes Alive After Collection

Before you dash down to a coral reef armed with collecting gear and (I hope) having read and remembered Chapter Four, take my advice and organize your equipment for storage depending on what you expect to catch. It is heart-breaking to have collected choice fishes and not have the wherewithal to keep them—far more heart-breaking than not being able to catch everything you see, which no one can, anyway.

If you are in a really remote spot without power for your aerators and filters, keep your fish in floating baskets or similar containers anchored in the sea. I designed a piece of equipment that is now widely used by Sri Lankan collectors. Basically, it is a large, soft, plastic 7-gallon bottle (used for transport of essences, acids, etc.). The top is cut off and it is liberally drilled with holes to permit ample water circulation. Around it is tied an old inner tube. It is better not to drill the bottom, although in so doing you can get rid of droppings and waste. It is sometimes necessary to drag this ashore and transfer your catch to another receptacle, so that if, say a foot of water remains, it does not drain out the bottom holes and leave your precious catch floundering about.

Many diver-collectors who do not have SCUBA gear tow these about with long lines attached to their waists and pop their catches in them.

Professionals anchor flotillas of them in the shallows. Thereby, they keep their specimens alive and healthy for days, or even weeks. Bear in mind that you should not put bullies or

In shallow water a floating bucket-and-tube arrangement keeps the catch fresh until time to move on.

incompatibles in the same container. These containers are usually cheap, collapsible, and light. You can use as many as you want; perhaps one for each choice fish if need be.

This cannot be done in very warm, shallow water, such as in the Red Sea during the summer. In this case, if

possible, anchor them in deeper water using a long anchor line and strong anchor. Cover them from seagulls and terns (which often rob from them).

A semi-permanent raft with multiple compartments I designed has given years of service. A wooden framework holds up to a dozen perforated, rigid, plastic canisters with cut tops in place. Each is tied to the framework with tough nylon or kuralon line. The front end, which is anchored, is shaped like a ship's bow to face the wind or current. Flotation is by several cylindrical Styrofoam pieces tied on the sides. A lid covered with strong fishing net gives protection from gulls and terns. It also prevents fish from jumping out. I can store a dozen good-sized tangs, angelfish, hundreds of damselfishes, and generally up to 500 choice marines in such an apparatus.

There is nothing quite like circulation of natural seawater as nature's cure for wounds, abrasions, ripped fins and coral cuts on newly-collected marines.

If for some reason you cannot do this, the next best thing (provided you have a power-supply) is to have a small pump bring seawater from the shallows into your containers for circulation. Otherwise use an aerator, but change the water twice a day.

The only other way of keeping fishes is to aerate them with oxygen. Except for tiny damsels and such, it is wisest to use one plastic bag per fish. Use suitably-sized plastic bags of fairly strong gauge, and always use two bags in case of leaks. The bag must be at least twice as wide as the fish is long, and the water must cover the fish completely. In the case of Moorish Idols, the long dorsal could be damaged without sufficient water to cover at least half of it.

Many fish become violent or aggressive when confined in bags. If bags are placed too close to each other, the fishes may suffer damage from spines when, for instance, two *Pomacanthus* are sparring through the transparent plastic. Because of this, it is wise to put newspaper in between the bags, or better still in between the two bags in which each fish is packed. This also shows up any minor leak when the paper turns damp and discolored.

Some collectors even go to the extent of using mild tranquilizers to keep their catches quiet after capture. It is not important to do this. If covered and kept in a dark, cool place, the captives soon settle down and rest.

It is very important to allow all fishes to defecate as soon as collected. They do this in minutes from fright anyway. However, you would be surprised as to how much waste matter is eventually dispelled and over how long a period. If a newly captured fish is placed in a bag and oxygenated at once, the water and oxygen must be changed

within six hours, and again at least six hours later. The algae-feeders, like tangs and angelfish, are the most prone to fouling their bags. Lionfishes and groupers usually disgorge their food, which must be removed immediately.

Triggerfishes and wrasses go into shock as soon as they are collected. It is necessary to give them very little oxygen, if any at all, or else they simply lie on their side, breathe more slowly and practically commit suicide. For these fishes, I prefer to use frequent water changes and aeration. If there is no power, use an aerator working off an automobile battery. The very last resort is to bleed compressed air off a SCUBA tank into the containers. Triggers and wrasses should not be packed in oxygen for at least six hours after capture, better yet 12.

Triggers present another problem. They bite their bags with vigor and spirit. Sri Lankan collectors have to imprison them first in well-perforated bags, which are then put into their water-filled plastic bags for oxygenation.

When filling a bag with oxygen, first crimp it to remove as much air as possible, then insert the nozzle of the oxygen cylinder into the neck of the bag, inflate it as much as possible and finally twist the neck of the bag. Bend it over once and tie it firmly with rubber bands.

Check your bags from time to time for leaks. If one has

collapsed considerably, it is leaking. It is simple to place it inside another good one and tie this over the top after adding more oxygen. A bag which leaks into its container (which should be, if possible, a plastic one) below the level of the oxygen, does not need instant attention if you are in a

Much of the gear used can be assembled on the diving site when needed. This is a mesh cage for holding fishes that have been collected. Photo by Rick Sammon.

hurry. The water levels equalize and if the oxygen remains in the bag, the fish is safe.

For fishes which may have suffered abrasions or fin damage during capture, it is important to treat the water in their bags with an antibiotic, particularly if it is to be stored for longer than about eight hours. An inexpensive water-soluble compound of penicillin is oftentimes adequate.

If you are obliged to store them for more than 48 hours after capture and prior to transport away from the collecting grounds, it may be necessary to feed the smaller fishes lightly—especially baby damsels and the like. Chopped clams or shrimp, or lobster or crab eggs will do. A very easy and cheap food almost always obtained in tropical waters is the ova of sea urchins. Most fishes love these eggs. They will gobble them up happily even in unhappy captive conditions.

If you apply the rule of one fish per bag or container for most fishes over 2 inches in size, you will have practically no casualties from fighting and damage. Even the tiny angelfish are belligerent creatures and are best packed by themselves, or else in aerated containers or floating canisters with many more of their own kind. This causes confusion whereby no one specimen is singled out for destruction.

One angelfish packed with a number of damsels will be fine. However, if it is placed with small butterflyfish it will start bullying them.

Tangs of the same species always fight and rip each other with their tail-spines. They are less prone to do this with other species.

Lionfish are very good-natured. They do not mind being packed together.

Too many marine catfishes, *Plotosus lineatus*, in one container will form a ball so tight as to smother those within. They soon die and foul the water.

Never put other fishes with boxfish, cowfish, and poison-exuding groupers, like *Grammistes sexlineatus* and *Diploprion bifasciatum.* These problem fishes should be rinsed in the sea in a net or in your gloved hand several times to get rid of as much of their poison as possible. They then are packed or accommodated singly and with more water than would be used for other

fishes of the same size.

Generally, fishes of almost the same size of the belligerent species, which are young or juvenile, will get along together in temporary storage. But adults, even of the same size, surely will fight. The clownfish are the most notorious.

There is no longer any need to transport fragile, heavy and expensive aquariums out to remote collecting areas. For many years, the most practical "aquariums" in the field have been wooden boxes or packing-cases lined with polyethelene bags. If one leaks, just put another new one inside it. I have seen collectors travelling from Singapore to Europe on large ocean vessels using containers of this type, with perfect results.

Dr. Herbert R. Axelrod photographing a freshly caught fish using his famous narrow glass photo tank method.

Transport From Point of Collection to Stocking Center

Depending on where you have collected your marines, the journey back to your permanent or semipermanent storage center where the fishes will be accommodated in immovable aquariums, could be by sea, air, rail or road. Packing for each mode of transportation varies considerably.

By sea, the problems are somewhat lessened, unless it is very rough and the intervening stretches of water are polluted. Where conditions are favorable, a sea journey for your captives can not only be inexpensive, but also could keep them in excellent shape. An area of deck space with an awning of canvas to keep out the direct sun is best. Accommodate the fishes in open plastic bags lying in wooden boxes or stiff plastic canisters with their tops cut off to give them plenty of space. Use an electric pump worked off the power supply of the boat to aerate the containers— but carry a spare, just in case. Also, have available oxygen and the wherewithal to oxygenate the fish if the sea gets rough or the power supply is interrupted.

You can change water using the ship's pumps or the more strenuous system of lowering a bucket into the sea. But be sure to tie one end of the long rope to the ship's rail!

Since you have all the seawater you will ever need, you can change it frequently and also be generous with the amount in each container. If there is considerable rolling and pitching, the fishes actually suffer distress with less water. On a memorable journey back from the Maldives, when I brought back alive a sizeable collection of choice marines to Colombo on the deck of a steamer, the casualties en route were due to "seasick" fishes!

Additional water in each container gives more cushion

Diver/Collector shows off one of his prize possessions after returning to shore.

to the shock from rough seas. More frequent changes remove the fouling, which tends to increase in such conditions.

In very rough, stormy weather, put them in containers with oxygen. Use plenty of water, changing only when the seas have subsided.

When you are approaching your destination, make sure that the seawater is unpolluted when you change it.

Air transport is expensive, but much quicker and probably the least bumpy, except when the weather is really turbulent. Packing in oxygen is the rule. It stands to reason that the least amount of water and packing material possible should be used. Styrofoam boxes of suitable sizes are now commercially available for the purpose. These are not only light and handy but also offer excellent insulation against heat and cold. Most important of all, they are leakproof in the event of a bag being damaged by fish. Airlines do not take kindly to clients whose fish cartons spring leaks in the cargo holds.

If you do not accompany the cargo and see it loaded, be sure to label each carton conspicuously to indicate which side is up and the perishability of the contents. Ensure, too, that it travels in a pressurized warm hold in the larger aircraft on journeys lasting more than six hours.

Unless you have your own charter, it is unlikely that fishes can be airlifted without packing them in oxygen. Air pumps working off aircraft power supplies are not available and hardly worth considering if oxygen is available. Make sure that oxygen is available at the point of capture for packing. No airline will agree to airlift full cylinders of oxygen or most gases, even compressed air, for obvious reasons. A private charter may do this with special permission.

Transport by road is possibly the only way to transport fishes in many locations. If loading them in a truck, oxygen packing is the most suitable and inexpensive procedure for hauls of up to 12 hours. It is useful to carry canisters of fresh seawater if the trip is overland without the possibility of an emergency change of water on the way. Check your cargo every six hours, if possible, for leaks and signs of distress.

Plastic containers are preferred, but if unavailable use stiff wax-treated cardboard cartons. Insulate with Styrofoam if passing through cold areas, and against the heat if travelling takes place at midday. The best time to travel is by night when there is usually less traffic and the air is much cooler.

Always take spare bags, oxygen, rubber bands and such.

You should pack more water per bag than you would for air transport because of the greater bumpiness of average tropical roads. This could cause some discomfort to your fishes if they are swished about too much and too often in their bags.

By rail (especially railways in the tropics), your packing should be safeguarded against meddling, pilferage and bad handling. Light wooden

boxes lined with Styrofoam pieces are best, with very clear labeling and tied in such a way that they are not carried upside

The box is packed as close to flight time as possible and is quickly on its way. Photo by Herbert R. Axelrod.

down or stowed in unsuitable freight cars. Inquisitive eyes and meddling fingers present the greatest hazard to fishes consigned by rail. Bumping is

less than by road, except for the occasional lurch at a station. Generally, the fishes travel quite well in this manner.

Generally, in packing for regional transport of marines, space for each specimen is the most vital consideration. It does not stand to reason that if, for instance, you pack 20 fishes individually in one box for a six-hour journey, you can put in 40 for 12 hours. On the other hand, you can cut down on water and weight for the longer journey because the volume of oxygen required is greater. This means also that you cut down on freight costs. Using more water on a short journey is not an extravagance, but rather a means of transporting your fishes to arrive in better condition and with less time spent acclimatizing them after capture. But do not carry this extravagance too far. Never put in more water by volume in a bag than oxygen. Half and half is about the limit. The average plastic bag will burst at its seams with too much water.

Make a table providing a generalized packing system for the more commonly collected tropical marines, as regards size, gauges of bag, volume of water and oxygen required. Using this as a guide, and with a little practice, you should be able to achieve a low casualty rate on your collecting expeditions.

Collecting in Tide Pools and Shallow Water

For non-swimmers, the elderly and the young, tide-pools and shallows in the tropics are safe and rewarding collecting grounds. When I was only 12, I caught an 8-inch *Pterois miles* in a tide-pool on a coral reef in South Sri Lanka and transferred it by hand into a bucket. How I was not stung I will never know. Nowadays I will not enter the water without gloves.

The serious tide-pool collectors should wear swim-trunks or shorts. In very dense corals, high-top sneak-ers or their equivalent are a must. If the intention is to spend several hours at this fascinating game, do not feel you will be laughed at for donning a long-sleeved shirt, levis and a wide-brimmed hat. The laughers will not stand in the hot sun for long. If they do, it will be your turn for a laugh in the evening when their sunscreen does not quite prevent them from turning very red and very hot.

If you have an assistant, try using a glass-bottomed bucket to help you see more clearly through the surface ripples. You will be amazed at the difference. Using one yourself and a net in the other hand works only for the very slow and easily collected fishes. If the pools are deep enough to get into, try a face-mask. When you have stopped wondering at the beauty of it all, you speedily will learn to swim and enroll yourself in a

diving club, learn SCUBA, and go all the way as thousands have done before you.

Although tide-pool collecting involves the use of nets for the most part, other appliances and methods are applicable. Tranquilizers or soporifics particularly are effective if the tide is low because of the restricted area and lack of currents. In the larger tide-pools, using ultra-light fishing tackle can get you a fine selection of wrasses and small groupers. Small baited minnow traps or wide-mouthed clear jars will tempt many smaller fishes to enter, whereupon you can block the mouth with your hand or net and bring up some interesting

captives. In tide-pools you almost always encounter juveniles and other smaller fishes. They are the amateur collector's delight.

At night you will be amazed at what turns up in tide-pools. The squirrelfishes, nearly all invisible by day, are out in force at night. With a powerful underwater flashlight you can net, without even swimming, a fair variety of them of proper size. Morays are out in the open too, and any *Pterois* not seen by day is out with fins outstretched in the dark and can be netted with ease.

Here is a list of species which are commonly collected in tide-pools in Sri Lanka. You can get an idea of what to expect in similar tropical or

Rodney Jonklaas shipped many thousands of fishes from Sri Lanka. B.O.A.C. was the carrier and even provided "fishmuffs" which insulated the live fishes from drastic temperature changes. Photo courtesy B.O.A.C.

semitropical locations and plan your collecting likewise:

Morays—*Echidna nebulosa, Gymnomuraena zebra, Uropterygius concolor* and *Gymnothorax favagineus*, all small and young.

Snake-eels—*Ophichthus sp.*

Squirrelfishes—*Sargocentron spinifer, S. diadema, Myripristis murdjan,* etc.

Groupers—*Grammistes sexlineatus,* young *Epinephelus fuscoguttatus.*

Flagtails—*Kuhlia taeniura.*

Goatfishes—many species.

Angelfishes—Juveniles of *Pomacanthus semicirculatus.*

purpurea, lunare, hardwicke, janseni, Halichoeres marginatus and *Hortulanus, Labroides dimidiatus.*

Parrotfishes—it is surprising at night, how large the parrotfishes are which nestle in among the corals and rocks in tide-pools, some of them in their gelatinous cocoons.

Blennies—most species prefer tide-pools.

Moorish Idols—*Zanclus canescens* often hides in rock-pools under ledges, and is easily collected by night.

Tangs—the most common tide-pool surgeonfish is

they obligingly creep into loose bits of coral lying on the sand bottom. Just take these chunks out and shake them into a bucket, or gently chop out the fish using a light hammer or axe.

Boxfish—*Ostracion cubicus* are common in tide-pools.

Canthigasters—*Canthigaster solandri* in small sizes frequent tide-pools.

In locations where the tide is greater than 2 feet, as in Singapore, it is all-important to operate only at low tide, but in Sri Lanka high tide often brings in hungry wrasses that can be hooked only at that time.

There are a few minor dangers to note. Poisonous fish, of course, are dangerous. Stinging hydroids growing underneath the corals and rocks (away from the light) should be avoided. Be wary of walking on fragile corals which may collapse with your weight and cause abrasions on your ankles. Also, big morays occasionally come in and can be dissuaded with a spear or light speargun.

Fish collectors often carry a camera with them while diving so as not to miss any "once-in-a-lifetime" photos. Photo by Jean Deas at Lord Howe Island.

Sometimes collecting fishes is relatively easy. Nets placed in shallow water may be all that is needed.

Butterflyfishes—Juveniles of *Chaetodon auriga, citrinellus, pictus, vagabundus, lunula, melannotus, trifascialis, collare, trifasciatus.*

Damselfishes—*Abudefduf saxatilis* and *sordidus, Pomacentrus* species and many others.

Wrasses—*Thalassoma*

Acanthurus triostegus, and it is caught easily, especially by night.

Lionfishes—*Pterois miles* and *radiata* often are collected in very shallow tide-pools.

Triggers—the only trigger that likes tide-pools is juvenile *Rhinecanthus aculeatus,* and when less than 2 inches long

The Diver-Collector without SCUBA

Not everyone can afford to own SCUBA gear. In the more remote parts of the tropical world, even if one can get hold of an outfit charging it from a high pressure compressor is seldom, if at all, possible.

At any rate, whether or not you are a collector, learning to skin-dive is a very necessary part of your training to eventually SCUBA dive. Once again, this book need hardly dwell on the finer points of skin-diving, training schedules, etc., because there are already so many comprehensive works on the market.

Let us assume that you are something of a swimmer. You need not be an expert swimmer in the competitive class, nor does your style and speed have very much bearing on your eventual prowess as a collector. It is sufficient if you are fit, healthy and confident. Above all else, you must possess common sense and exercise caution.

Many of the finest skin-diver collectors I know never had swimming training, and a good many professionals make a great deal more money outwitting elusive coral fishes than the average swimming-pool instructor.

To be able to collect marines effectively, you must wear a face mask of your choice, flippers, a snorkel if you feel it is useful and, of course, gloves. If you are buoyant, you will do better with weights. Then you will not waste too much energy getting down, and staying down while both hands are engaged in cornering and netting a fish.

The basic principle in skin-diving with a hand net, especially by day, is to bring the fish to your net. Bear this in mind and you will be successful a lot sooner than if you try to bring the net to the fish.

By night it is just the opposite. You blind or dazzle your target with a powerful flashlight and bring the net to him.

A skin-diver can use nets, traps, light angling tackle, or tranquilizers to collect fish. By being in the same element as the fish and being able to see underwater, the diver has a great advantage over the tide-pool collector or wader.

Let's discuss nets. There are dozens of different kinds now in use. Most of them are lovingly fashioned by the divers and collectors themselves. They can be classified as follows:

1. Hand nets
2. Set nets
3. Lift nets
4. Chaser nets

HAND-NETS

Forget the kinds of nets you buy in pet shops and your favorite aquarium store. These are strictly for use in aquariums and ponds. On the reefs, you need an instrument that is light, corrosion-proof, fast and with sufficient "bag" to enclose (not to enmesh or entangle) your catch.

Remember, you are going to

One safety measure when diving is to make sure the anchor is secure. Divers do not want to surface to find that their boat has drifted away. Photo by R. Taylor.

capture desirable, most often delicate, fishes unlike the professional fisherman who is after something to kill and eat. Every effort should be made to avoid injury to the fish. The material used should be the softest nylon or similar fabric. Cotton is all right, but it rapidly rots away and is easily torn. In an emergency, a few choice fishes have been collected by enterprising divers

use up to four different types of nets which can more or less catch almost any fish which is nettable.

The largest net which can be used by an average skin-diver is a spade-shaped or rectangular net with $^1/_4$ inch aluminum wire framework. The material used is $^3/_8$ to $^1/_4$ inch four-ply nylon netting. The "bag" is as deep as the handle is long and the bottom

wide, with a handle about 8 inches in length. It is very effective for collecting species of *Amphiprion, Dascyllus, Pomacentrus, Plotosus* and the like in one sweep. If two divers operate with one chasing while the other nets, up to 20 or more individuals of *Pomacentrus* can be captured in one breath lasting less than 30 seconds! This is economical and effective collecting at

The famous One Tree Island, Great Barrier Reef, Australia. The dark blue area is deep water, the lighter blue behind the island is the shallow lagoon. Photo by Dr. Gerald R. Allen.

who filched pieces of mosquito netting from their lodgings! A hand net is one that is wielded by the diver using one hand. This means that the length of the handle and weight and size of the net are limited. Some of the most proficient collectors

does not end in a cone. It is sewn in a straight line the same length of the net. The material should be colored brown, blue or green, never white.

This net measures 3 to 5 ft. in length. It is 12 to 18 inches

its professional best. *Pomacentrus coelestis* can be collected this way and it is called "blueing" or "blueherding." One soon learns to pick the best time and spot for such an operation. A net of this type is not much good at night, except for shoals of *Plotosus lineans*, which literally can be decimated with one.

The idea of not having a cone-shaped bag is to keep the fishes separate from each other as much as possible when bringing the catch to the surface and handing it over to someone for transfer into a container.

A very popular hand net is a smaller version of the above that is nearly always spade-shaped, unless specially designed for use in a harbor with straight walls, where a rectangular one is more effective. The average "day net," as it is called, is about 18 inches long, 10 inches wide, with a handle of about 8 inches and a "bag" of not more than 12 inches in depth. The usual mesh is $1/4$ inch nylon, three ply, colored brown or green. I once experimented with a pink one and found that anemonefishes are not too wary of it. Black is suitable and even more effective by night. An effective day net has the same measurements, but a larger mesh to give it speed and maneuverability. A fast one is used for chasing and cornering fishes, like *Chaetodon, Forcipiger*, etc., where very often sheer speed and quick movements are necessary. It is necessary to avoid a mesh size which could result in a fish being gilled. Gilled specimens seldom recover and are best released if caught in this fashion.

Night nets are usually smaller and rounded in shape, although on moonlit nights, when the fishes can see you and take evasive action requiring some pursuit, you may have to resort to day

Push nets are handy when a single person is collecting. They are simple but efficient when wielded by an experienced collector. Photo of Gerson Epstein by Dr. Herbert R. Axelrod.

nets, usually the fast black-meshed ones. An average night net has a diameter of 10 inches and a handle longer than usual, up to 14 inches. The longer handle is often useful when thrusting the net

under ledges and caves to capture hiding *Acanthurus* and *Pomacanthus*. In very dense coral, an even longer handle is necessary. Generally, a night net is made of stronger nylon, from 4-ply to

8-ply, as strength and ruggedness, rather than speed and maneuverability, are the requirements. The "bag," too, can be longer than usual.

Additional gear that is useful when collecting are wet suits (or at least a wet suit top), a weight belt, and a probe of some sort. Photo by Rodney Jonklaas.

circular net about 6 feet in diameter, with lead weights all around it. Rexie chases baby *Acanthurus lineatus* and various butterflyfishes into coral or boulders with many

to accept bait laid on the bottom. It is simply a collapsible, rectangular framework with netting inside. It is laid on the sea bottom with four lines, one at each corner, joined to one that reaches to the surface and is kept up by a float. One baits the bottom over the net and swims on the surface looking downward. When enough fishes have gotten into the net, it is speedily raised with its captives. It is seldom used in some countries, but should prove useful for baby *Coris* and other wrasses.

SET NETS

A "set net" is one that is installed in place and fishes are driven or coaxed into it. Large set nets are seldom, if ever, used. They necessitate more than two divers to operate. The time taken and the injury to fishes collected in them are such that they are hardly worthwhile. A small version, affectionately called a "moxie," is a popular net greatly relied on by a few skillful collectors. The original "moxie" was invented by Mr. Rex Mortier, popularly named "Rexie." Rexie is not a fast or deep diver, but he gets great hauls with his "moxie." It is a

entrances and exits. He then drapes his "moxie" over the entire formation and dives down with an old tine which he beats underwater. The noise drives the fishes out of their hiding places and into the "moxie." There is no better way of getting small *Acanthurus lineatus* and *leucosternon*. In diver-collectors' parlance, to go out "moxieing" is an accepted form of collecting baby *Acanthurus* by day.

LIFT NETS

A lift net is a European invention. I sometimes works on fishes which can be lured

CHASER NETS

A "chaser net" often is used by solo diver-collectors in conjunction with a standard "day net." The chaser net is very long-handled and light, with a small diameter and "bag." The material used is usually white. The main purpose of a chasernet is to frighten a moving fish into the main net. The long handle doubles as a probe in case the fish dives into a hole. This probing is called "tickling." A simple, long aluminum rod of from 2 to 4 ft. is called a "tickler." In a very small hole or crevice, the net end of the chaser often comes in handy for netting a cornered specimen. It also is useful to collect the cleaner shrimps *Stenopus hispidus* and *Lysmata grabhami*.

A solo diver-collector seldom tows along a floating, perforated container for his catches if he has no attendant boat. For this purpose, he hires a friend, usually a beginner or trainee, who is called a "tube-pusher" or "tube-master," because the usual flotation for such a container is an old automobile tube.

The solo collector keeps his catch in either a small plastic or aluminum container, with suitable perforations and snap-lid, tied around his waist. Some use up to four separate polyethylene bags, each one for a different species of fish. There should be at least two, because species like boxfish and *Grammistes sexlineatus* cannot be kept with other fishes, which they immediately poison to death.

A really enterprising collector puts a lot of faith in his gloves. I am fastidious, almost fanatic, about them. I have suffered countless stings, bites and abrasions in the course of collecting for many years.

My favorite gloves are made of nylon. They extend up to within a few inches of my elbows and have elastic at the wrist and at the edge of the open end. As I am left-handed, the right-hand glove used to frighten or chase is white, while the left-hand glove is brown or a neutral shade. I find leather or rubber gloves quite hopeless and clumsy. The fingers must be as free as possible to get maximum ease of movement. Very often a well-cornered fish is extracted from a crevice by hand. As a matter of fact, most triggers are collected by hand and few divers dare to do this without gloves.

At night it is not possible to use two nets simultaneously, since one hand is used to carry your underwater flashlight. Nor are bags or containers around your waist convenient. One must use a floating container or work off a boat. The average diver-

A common method of collecting in the Philippines is to surround an area with a "fence net" and use hand nets within the fenced off region. Photo by Dr. Don E. McAllister.

collector without SCUBA works in water from 6 to 30 feet deep. The really expert ones often go deeper. However, experience has shown that many fish brought up suddenly and swiftly from water deeper than, say 25 feet, suffer distress from distended swim-bladders and often die unless relieved. This will be dealt with in more detail in the next chapter.

The average skin-diving collector operates in depths up to 30 feet, but prefers 15 feet where it is not too shallow and not deep enough for some fishes to be distressed by bladder distension. Very shallow water is not easy to work in because the fishes are unusually wary during the

day. At night, the shallower the better. If you can hold your breath consistently for 45 seconds on a dive and work for up to four hours in water averaging 20 feet in depth, you compare favorably with some of the leading professionals; at least in endurance. But the volume and nature of your catch also is dependent on your experience, speed, intelligence and maneuverability under water, and of course on the weather and sea conditions.

It is best to go out specifically for fishes you require and not try to catch everything you fancy. To concentrate on one or a few worthwhile species usually brings better results.

The SCUBA Diving Collector

Learn to SCUBA dive and you widen your underwater collecting horizons to include dozens of previously unattainable species. You can work deeper and longer than if you were just snorkeling and can observe so much more of the life on a tropical reef.

Be sure to go through a course in SCUBA diving and at least for the first few days, or always, take along a buddy. Although I am a "loner" through force of circumstances, I would unhesitatingly advise all SCUBA diving collectors to adhere to the buddy system. This is mainly for safety's sake, but that person can also help with the collecting of the fishes and can share in some of life's great adventures.

Your equipment is basically the same when collecting with SCUBA, but with several embellishments. You can take several nets down with you and several larger containers. You can even carry plastic squeeze-bottles of tranquilizers, light traps, hammers or small crowbars, and considerable gadgetry. If you have buddies, so much the better. They can follow you around with most of this equipment!

And if you SCUBA dive by night, you are perhaps the most effective instrument of tropical fish collecting in a selective and humane fashion ever devised.

Since you are slower wearing SCUBA than without, you require more stealth and a knowledge of fishes' habits than when operating from the surface. But since you can stay down for a long time, any

fish that is cornered or trapped is yours in due course.

Many fishes are sensitive to sudden changes in water pressure and here is a list of them:

Squirrelfishes
Groupers*
Sea-perches*
Snappers
Adult angelfishes*
Adult butterflyfishes*
Adult surgeonfishes*
Lionfishes*
Boxfishes*
Canthigasters*
Big triggers

For these fishes, particularly those over 3 inches long , great care must be taken to bring them up slowly and in stages to overcome bladder distension. If the fish is brought up too fast, the swimbladder expands within the body wall and exerts pressure on the digestive system and other organs. The fish dies almost immediately or recovers very slowly if put back in a perforated container into deep water, kept there for up to half and hour, and then brought up very slowly, at the rate of approximately a foot per minute. This takes time, but it is worth it.

I sometimes have used a hypodermic syringe on distressed fish and released gas from their bladders. This gives them immediate relief from buoyancy and permits them to

---

* **Extra-sensitive to water presssure change.**

swim right side up instead of floating belly upwards. It is very important when inserting the syringe through the body wall into the bladder to avoid puncturing any other organs. It is useful to carry a syringe in the boat when you are diving deep for such fishes. Also dab the wound with antiseptic before putting it back in a container. However, experience has proven that whether or not you resort to a hypodermic needle it is better to bring sensitive fish up slowly and carefully at the rate of about a foot per minute. There will be no immediate casualties as may be experienced if you do this swiftly. Often there is no need at all for the hypodermic. The larger the fish, the tougher the bladder wall and the more sensitive it is to a drop in pressure.

An 8 inch *Cephalopholis miniatus* (one of the loveliest of groupers, but perhaps the most bladder-sensitive of all marine tropicals) will necessitate at least one hour of gradual decompression from a depth of 40 feet to the surface.

Your underwater fish containers should be somewhat more complicated and rugged than those you would use when snorkeling. Although the great Capt. Cousteau's collectors used transparent bags for this purpose when working in the Red Sea, I strongly advise against them, except for purposes of photography of the diver and his catch. Putting a fresh-caught marine tropical in a transparent bag gives it an immediate desire to escape, which speedily exhausts the fish. It also causes abrasions of the snout and fins, which manifest themselves in wounds later in tank conditions. Frantic fishes in bags also attract eager predators, like groupers and morays, which can not only rip the bags, but also give you headaches.

Put your captured marines into a container that is: 1) wide-mouthed, but also has a snap-lid which will not open underwater even if the latch comes off; 2) of strong, corrosion-proof material, like plastic or aluminum; 3) adequately perforated to permit circulation of seawater in and out of it; 4) light weight; 5) easily spotted, even in murky water; and 6) negatively buoyant.

By and large, I have found that aluminum milk cans of 2 to 4 gallon capacity are the ideal underwater fish containers. I have owned two for well over 12 years. Although battered and dented, they still serve me well. They have traveled with me to the Maldives, India and Malaysia, and have accommodated thousands of dollars worth of choice marines.

The typical fish container should have a lid of at least 5 inches diameter with a hinge and locking device. To make it snap down and stay down, I attach strong rubber bands on the inside, some distance away from the center, to enable a sizeable fish to be thrust inside it. One of my newer containers was fashioned from an aluminum bottle in which some essence or perfume concentrate was imported. I removed the tiny lid and cut an 8 inch diameter

hole in the top. I then fitted on an aluminum lid of a saucepan which fits inside the aperture, although it opens outwards. (The handle of such a can need not be of aluminum.) Remove it and use strong nylon cord instead. Then there is less rattle on a rough day under water.

My pet outfit is an aluminum can together with at least one plastic wide-mouth jar attached to it with what I call a "decompression" line. This is a length of strong nylon cord at least $1/4$ inch in diameter wound around a bright plastic float.

When working in deep water and anticipating having to bring fishes up slowly to the boat, I use up to 60 feet of decompression cord held in

place on the float with a rubber band. When I have finished collecting and the air in my SCUBA tank is almost over, I remove the rubber band. This causes the float to rush upwards and unravel the decompression cord. If I am some distance away, my boatman rushes up to me to take charge of the float. This enables me to get into the boat for a rest and an exchange of tanks.

In very calm water I do not wind my cord. I operate with the float on the surface, thus marking my position for my buddies and the boat. When it is choppy, it is better to release the float toward the end of the dive.

The wide-mouthed plastic container attached to the

Some animals are dangerous to handle. This diver is carefully showing off the two dorsal fin spines of a Port Jackson Shark (*Heterodontus portusjacksoni*); these can cause a lot of damage to an unwary collector. Photo by Walter Deas.

main one serves two purposes. First, it tends to float, thereby marking the spot if the main one has fallen into a crevice and is not readily spotted. Often, one has to relinquish containers and concentrate only on the fish you are chasing. The chase goes on for several minutes and may lead you quite some

In really murky water I like to release the float at the beginning. This way I can relocate containers after a chase by merely going to the surface, spotting the float and going down along the line to the container.

Seldom is a very big net used with SCUBA, unless it is a concentrated two-man effort

underwater and, without letting its captives escape, add another elusive fish to it. I usually select a good spot well away from urchins and anemones. I then hold the can between my knees, open the lid with one hand and thrust net and captive into the apparatus, blocking the entrance completely. If the fish is suitably sized (and not a stinging one like *Pterois*), it can be caught by gloved hand from the net and thrust into the can. Never handle a fish with thumb and forefinger. Use all your fingers and hold it gently all around, or cup it in the palm of your hand.

Inside a dark can, your captives will be less frantic than if put in a plastic bag. At the same time they will defecate. So, from time to time tilt the container to let the droppings fall out from the ventilation holes. If you have a large fish like a

One of the most difficult habitats to collect in is the coral reef. Imagine chasing a small fish among these corals! Torn nets and broken coral often result from such attempts. Photo by Dr. Leon P. Zann.

distance from the container. It is essential that you waste as little air as possible relocating it. Hence, the plastic container becomes a kind of underwater marker. Second, this container can also house delicate invertebrates and sometimes a poison-exuding fish which cannot be kept in the main one.

for damselfish. It is not easy to transfer a bunch of small fishes from a big net into a container without having several escape from the container and from the net. A big net is best emptied at the surface or by an assistant in a boat.

It takes a little practice and dexterity to open a container

grouper in it, smaller captives like clowns will hover near the lid. You have to be especially careful not to let them escape when trying to put in another captive.

It is quite surprising how many fishes will be accommodated in a can without injury. They are not in a mood to attack each other, nor can they see well enough to hurt themselves trying to escape. They spend most of their time defecating—which is precisely what you want them to do!

In succeeding chapters I will describe and discuss methods of collecting with SCUBA other than with hand-nets. In the one, netting is the main method. All nets I have described in Chapter Eight can be adapted for use with SCUBA.

For such species as *Chaetodon mertensii, Cephalopholis miniatus, Pseudanthias squamipinnis, Nemateleotris magnifica* and juvenile *Pomacanthus imperator*, SCUBA diving with a net is the only practical method of capture. They are all fairly deep-diving fishes and elusive. Only a super breath-holder has any kind of hope of getting an occasional specimen without SCUBA. At night, diving with SCUBA is very effective indeed.

Twin-tank SCUBA is the most effective type of gear for night work. During the day a single tank unit is better than a double tank. This is because you often have to move fast to chase an elusive fish. This is true also on moonlit nights.

On a dark, calm, clear night, you virtually have the entire visible population of a coral reef at your mercy with the correct nets, cans and a powerful flashlight. Transferring captives into a can by night is a little trickier than by day. I usually drop the nets and grip the can between my knees. I hold the flashlight under an armpit and direct it towards the lid.

Damselfishes are among the many fishes that use coral stands for shelter when danger threatens. They will move up into open water to snatch plankton but will retreat to the corals if a predator appears. Photo by Dr. Gerald R. Allen.

I then open the can and thrust net and captive into it. I gently pull back the net and let the lid snap shut.

More than by day, at night it is useful to have a good marker for your can, both underwater and above. Carry your containers along with you wherever you go searching for fish. As soon as you spot one you want drop the can and get to work.

It is imperative that you work from a boat at night. If you are very close to shore and in suitably deep water, have an assistant with a flashlight to guide you when you are on the surface and

out of air, ready to bring in your catch.

I am not happy working in very deep water at night in tropical seas, especially alone, as I usually am! Having a buddy helps, but ask him not to flash his light on you. This will reveal you to the fish you want to catch.

I do not dive deeper than 30 feet at night. Even from this depth, where I collect a good many choice specimens, like *Acanthurus leucosternon*, I find it useful to bring the captives up slowly, say at a rate of about 3 feet per minute.

Spearfishing for Live Marines

Most readers will imagine that I have devised some kind of a hypodermic spearhead which will inject a sleeping drug into a fish and hence aid in its capture. This is done, as a matter of fact, with big fishes for oceanariums. It seems to be the only effective way of collecting big groupers, rays and sharks. We are not, however, concerned with big fishes.

If you want to collect at least two species which live in close association with larger fishes (or turtles), the remora (*Echeneis naucrates*) and the juvenile golden crevalle (*Gnathanodon speciosus*), being proficient at spearfishing helps.

The remora spends most of its time attached to sharks and other predatory fishes. They are most often found attached to queenfish (*Scomberoides lysan*), which are much sought after by fishermen. Many of them carry one or two medium-sized remoras on them. If they are hooked, or speared, the persistent remoras often can be netted off their bodies before being boated.

I collect a few remoras this way each season. They are wonderful pets for the aquarium. They constantly are in demand from dealers.

It is important to spear the host fish in a vital spot so that it does not struggle too violently. In which case, the remora lets go and swims around looking for another host. I have observed that most fishes do not like carrying remoras. They do their

best to avoid remoras that are on the lookout for a free ride and free meals.

On a few occasions, I have pretended to be a host. I actually have lured remoras to my own body and netted them. Perhaps they thought I was some weird form of bubbling dugong. Wearing SCUBA, one can stay down longer and try to look enticing

to a hostless remora.

One morning I was out collecting and spearfishing with one of my young co-divers, Tony Schuilling. We had some fine sport with queenfish. After this I donned a SCUBA tank and went down with net and cans for smaller marines. I saw three obviously lonely little remoras swimming around close to the

Small submersibles fitted with video cameras are helpful in scouting out areas before divers enter the water. Of course only sophisticated commercial collectors can afford such luxuries. Photo by Courtney Platt.

bottom. They were looking eagerly at me. Their hosts had been taken by us and were in the boat above.

"Tony," I said when I reached the surface, "I'm going down and net these remoras by offering myself to them."

Back on the bottom at only 20 feet, I swam as enticingly as I could. I imitated a porpoise with my flippered feet. In a minute I felt a cold object on my thigh. I swung my hand-net in the spot and was rewarded with a wriggling remora! Tony was genuinely impressed, more so when I went down again and got another. The third got smart and vanished, no doubt hitching a ride on a queenfish.

From then on I never missed a chance of collecting remoras in this fashion. They prefer sharks, but sharks are rather uncommon in some waters. At any rate, they are not easily approached and speared. Look for remoras on crevalle, cobia, amberjacks and similar fish. If you are not already a spearfisherman, ask a buddy who is good at it to help you collect them.

The baby golden crevalle is a much sought-after aquarium fish in the Indo-Pacific. Where it is found, the very small ones of about an inch in length often are found swimming with skin-divers and, then too, in front of their noses. If anyone tells you that they caught a few baby golden crevalle by swishing a net in front of their dive masks, don't laugh. But the slightly larger ones, from 2 to 4 inches, are found with groupers, large *Diodon* or *Tetraodon* and turtles, but most often with groupers. With a little experience, a diver can judge the size

of a grouper by the size of the golden crevalle hovering about its cave. When you see a golden crevalle of about 8 inches in size, the host grouper is well over 100 lbs.

If you are lucky enough to spot a host fish by night, netting the young crevalle from off its body is a cinch. One night in Colombo harbor I found a sleeping turtle. On its back were up to 20 young crevalle, of which I got 15 in one sweep of my net.

When a host fish has been speared, it must be drawn up rather slowly toward the boat and left underwater until the diver gets ready with a net. The

bigger the net, the better. If you can enclose the entire grouper, you have every crevalle that is around it. If you fail to net a few, chances are they will take fright and leave the spot to find another host. By the time the crevalle are about 8 inches or so, they are ready to swim away and fend for themselves. Often when collecting corals and invertebrates with SCUBA, and in the process turning over rocks, I have had hungry, friendly, young crevalle swim up to me and accompany me, not too closely, picking up tidbits on the way. They are impossible to net underwater at this stage.

Spearfishing cannot be used as a collecting tool except when the collector is after smaller fishes associated with the large ones that are speared, for example remoras or Golden Crevalle. This wrasse was probably speared for food. Photo by R. Taylor.

Fish-Traps

There are scores of different fish traps now in use all over the tropics and subtropics. Originally designed for food fish, a good many are now put out specifically for smaller ornamental marines. They range from simple, wide-mouth bottles, plastic minnow traps, and the woven cane traps of the Indian Ocean and Caribbean Sea, to the immense "kelongs" of Malaysia. The latter also are man-made islands of wood on which families live and fish for months on end.

Hundreds and thousands of choice marine tropicals are collected in traps. Although many are damaged and the casualty rate is high, the fact remains that for some species this is the most effective way of obtaining them.

There are two main categories of traps. Luck plays a big part in the "blind type." With the "visual type," divers work in conjunction with them which is an effective method of collecting choice marines.

BOTTLES

You would be quite surprised as to the effectiveness of strong wide-mouthed bottles as fish catchers, especially if you use them in conjunction with skin-diving gear or at least a glass-bottomed bucket. Most fishes cannot comprehend glass as an impenetrable material and, apart from being slightly suspicious of the edges and mouth of a wide-mouthed gallon jam jar, more often than not rush into it after bait.

Several years ago I placed considerable faith in strong jam jars as fish catchers, before I started night diving in earnest.

I used to collect many choice butterflyfishes, wrasses, and other species by simply baiting a jam jar and swimming over it until such time as a fish got in to gobble the food, whereupon I rushed down and closed the mouth with a net or my gloved hand before the captive found its way out. This works like a charm in water up to 20 feet deep and sufficiently clear for the jar to be observed from the surface. You can use SCUBA and stay quietly a discreet distance away from your trap, and then rush in and close the mouth when there are fish in it.

The larger the bottle, the better, within reason. But try to keep the mouth less than 6 inches in diameter to prevent large and hungry fishes dashing in and dispersing the bait.

When the bottom is unsuitable for the netting of *Pomacentrus* in the manner described in a previous chapter, use a bottle trap with shrimp, crab meat, urchin eggs, or chopped octopus or cuttlefish as bait and you will get fine results. For years I depended on bottles for my supply of *Pomacentrus coelestis* from the murky waters of Colombo harbor. In the same manner, I collected *Chaetodon pictus, Heniochus acuminatus, Thalassoma lunare, T. janseni* and other wrasses, *Paracirrhites forsteri,* many species of *Pomacentrus* and even an angelfish or two. The best thing about a bottle or plastic trap is that your captives are always in first-class condition. I even collected beautiful *Lutjanus sebae,* which had been rendered net-shy by other divers, by resorting to a big bottle and baiting it with their favorite food, urchin eggs.

PLASTIC TRAPS

The plastic minnow trap sold in most tackle stores works quite well for tropical marines, but if you can build your own with plexiglass and design it to suit marines, so much the better. A funnel entrance is useful if you leave your baited trap on the bottom and swim elsewhere and return to it later. Laying a series of plastic traps of this nature on a good bottom can yield many choice fishes and a good many surprises. In shallower water they don't work as well. But often even non-swimmers can use them "blind" and pull out beauties by using the proper bait. There is no bait quite so sought after as a slightly rotten prawn or shrimp.

The one disadvantage that plastic traps have is their lightness. This causes them to move under water in a swell. Fish will avoid anything which moves, so it may be useful to weight it down with rocks or coral. The plastic trap also should be kept clean and polished. Scratches on it make would-be intruders more wary than usual.

If you make your own plexiglass trap, choose a

square or a rectangular shape. This enables it to rest on most any bottom without rolling. It also enables easy spotting of any captives from the top or any angle underwater. A round or cylindrical shape is unsuitable, but if you add a funnel entrance this must be round.

You even can fashion an entrance to suit the fishes you need and obstruct others which are undesirable. A slit-shaped entrance ensures that only butterflyfish and fishes with slim outlines can enter. Also, it does not permit the undesirables, such as big groupers, boxfish and puffers.

PROFESSIONAL FISH TRAPS

In many parts of the tropical world, fishermen have devised traps for catching fishes as food. It is astounding to observe that in such widely separated areas as the Pacific Islands, South India, and the Caribbean, cane or wicker traps have followed an almost identical design. This is basically a flat-bottomed and flat-topped basket of wicker with a funnel-like entrance. There are scores of variations connected with mesh size, angle of funnel mouth, height, and length.

The smallest ones I know of are made in northeastern Sri Lanka with cane, but now replaced with stronger chicken-run mesh for conve-

nience. Tropical fish collectors prefer the cane because there is less injury to the captives. The mesh size is about 1 inch and the entrance is less than 6 inches, thereby enabling quite small marine tropicals to be collected.

The largest portable traps I have seen are immense cane cages in the South China Sea off the coast of Malaysia. These measured about 10 feet in length and 10 feet in height, with a mesh size of about 6 inches. They could be entered easily by a human being underwater. They were hauled to the surface with winches from sizeable fishing boats of the trawler class. I understood that they were

In rugged terrain fish traps are often useful. They must be checked regularly and the fishes removed promptly to prevent damage to their catch. Photo by Dr. Gerald R. Allen, Florida Island, Solomon Islands.

examined about once a week. Mostly food fishes of large size enter these unbaited traps. One or two I examined had the exquisite *Lo vulpinus* in them. This is possibly the way in which the trade gets its specimens.

Fish traps are made quite easily. Although I am not sure of this, there could be commercial plastic models now in use which are very effective indeed. The idea is to lure a fish inside with bait and make it set an example to others who follow for the bait, for companionship, through sheer curiosity, or to eat the captives.

An average trap ideally should measure about 4 feet in length and a foot high. It is usually made of cane or wickerwork, with a wooden frame and funnel entrance. It can be baited with stale bread, marine algae, chopped shells, mussels, or squid, depending on what fish are sought.

Some professionals do not use glass-bottomed buckets or masks for the most part. Where the water is murky, they fish "blind" so to speak, but bring up remarkable hauls. They care nothing about bladder distension, so that a good many choice specimens seldom make it alive to the surface if the traps are deeper than 30 feet. Even if they do, their chances of survival are poor.

If you can work in con- junction with professional trap fishermen, you stand to have better results. Divers who co-operate with trap fishermen use their underwa- ter vision to find the best spots and re-locate temporarily lost traps. The fishermen themselves know the best baits for what they want to trap. An intelligent collector can see to it that entrapped fish are pulled up slowly and carefully, and removed from the trap with skill and care. The usual method is to untie the string or fiber lashings on one side of it and collect the struggling captives by hand. As I stated earlier, the cane or wooden traps are better in that they cause less damage to the fishes than wire-netting ones.

At any rate, fishes taken from traps are best kept floating in the sea to recover from their abrasions. If put in aquaria, it is wise to add some antibiotic to prevent the wounds from becoming in- fected. The common areas of damage are on the forehead and lips.

Baiting traps is something of an art. Here are a few tips:

1. *Bread*—Stale bread attracts most fishes, especially tangs, parrotfishes, and butterflyfish. The color of white bread has a lot to do with it, but its relative crum- bliness is a disadvantage. The staler and whiter, the better.

2. *Chopped Shells*—The most popular is *Telescopium telescopium*, a common Indo- Pacific gastropod, which is broken and placed inside traps. These attract all man- ner of fishes, including the more carnivorous species, like wrasses, snappers and trig- gers.

3. *Marine Algae*—Big

A parrotfish and a Clown Triggerfish (*Balistoides conspicillum*) swim among the corals of Spur Reef, Great Barrier Reef. Photo by Dr. Gerald R. Allen.

bunches of fairly dense marine algae in season are used in traps. Although this attracts fishes, like the rabbitfish (Siganidae), others also come in. Moorish Idols are fond of algae and also several butterflyfishes and tangs.

4. *Jellyfish*—Big, firm jellies like *Aurelia*, when in season, often end up in traps. They attract butterflyfishes, siganids, tangs and the like.

5. *Squid or Cuttlefish*—Only the carnivorous fishes come in after these, but a few of them are choice, like *Lutjanus sebae*. But don't be surprised to find groupers and morays as well.

6. *Small fish*—Bunches of small sardines or herrings tied on the roof of the trap and hanging downward lure many species into traps. In fact, most baits, except the *Telescopium* shells, are suspended in this fashion. Here again, mostly the carnivores are attracted, especially groupers.

Live small fishes or any marine live bait, like wrasses, shrimp or crabs, are infinitely better. The problem is to confine them in the traps. This was overcome long ago by an intelligent fisherman who put them in clear glass bottles with perforated lids and suspended them from the roofs of the traps. The bait remained alive and wriggling safe in the bottles while the traps soon became full of eager, large-mouthed fish trying to swallow the bait!

7. *Broken Chinaware*—Try tossing some bits and pieces of white chinaware in a trap and await results. You will be astonished at the success of this foolproof method. The

"bait" lasts almost forever. Dozens of different species get in to examine it more closely or join their entrapped fellows through curiosity.

Here are the more outstanding regularly trap-collected marines:

Abalistes stellaris—adults up to 6 inches, mollusc bait.

Abudefduf saxatilis—adults in large numbers in each trap, mollusc bait.

Acanthurus leucosternon—adults, with bread or algae bait.

Acanthurus lineatus—average to adult size, bread or

Damselfishes are among the most common fishes seen swimming about a coral reef. This is the outer reef drop-off at Florida Island, Solomon Islands. Photo by Dr. Gerald R. Allen.

algae bait.

Acanthurus triostegus—average to adult size, bread or algae bait.

Antennarius—seasonally, enter traps after other fishes are already caught.

Apolemichthys xanthurus—occasionally, any bait.

Balistapus undulatus—all sizes, mollusc or small dead fish bait.

Canthigaster solandri—occasionally.

Centropyge multispinis—occasionally.

Chaetodon auriga—often, any bait.

Chaetodon falcula—seasonally, mollusc bait.

Chaetodon kleinii—often, mollusc bait or even bread.

Chaetodon gardneri—occasionally, mollusc bait.

Rubble areas are easier to collect in than large stands of coral. A net for fencing in the area would be useful here. Even then the fishes often escape through holes or tunnels through the loose coral. Photo by Dr. Gerald R. Allen, Guadalcanal, Solomon Islands.

Chaetodon meyeri—fairly often, adults only, mollusc or bread bait.

Chaetodon plebeius—occasionally, any bait.

Chaetodon trifascialis—occasionally, mollusc bait.

Chaetodon trifasciatus—often, any bait.

Chaetodon xanthocephalus—occasionally, any bait.

Coris gaimard—occasionally, mollusc bait.

Dendrochirus zebra—seasonally, after small fishes already entrapped, and for shelter.

Diploprion bifasciatum—often, after small fishes already entrapped.

Gomphosus varius—often, adult males only, mollusc bait.

Hemigymmus fasciatus—often, mollusc bait; trapping is probably the only method of collecting this fish.

Heniochus acuminatus—often, any size, mollusc bait.

Lutjanus kasmira—often, mollusc or fish bait.

Lutjanus malabaricus—often, mollusc or fish bait.

Lutjanus sebae—often, mollusc or fish bait.

Melichthys ringens—very commonly on mollusc bait.

Naso lituratus—adults, often, on algae bait.

Odonus niger—in large numbers, mollusc bait.

Plectorhinchus gaterinus—often, after any bait.

Plectorhinchus lineatusm—often, after any bait.

Pomacanthus imperator—occasionally, algae and bread bait.

Pomacanthus semicirculatus—often, adults only on algae bait, or even mollusc bait.

Sufflamen chrysopterus—often, mollusc bait.

Thalassoma lunare—adults, often on mollusc bait.

Thalassoma jansenii—adults, occasionally on mollusc bait.

Zanclus canescens—very commonly with algae or bread bait.

Zebrasoma desjardinii—occasionally with algae or mollusc bait.

Zebrasoma scopas—often, with algae bait.

Angling with Light Tackle

An astonishing number of quite nice tropical marines are caught by anglers. A few species can be collected only in this manner with any degree of certainty. Contrary to popular belief, a hooked fish does not die as a matter of course, and a barbless hook is not necessary to ensure quick removal. Modified or filed-down barbs are, in fact, essential.

There are two main forms of angling for aquarium specimens:

1. "Blind" angling, where the fisherman is in a boat or standing on land or on a reef without his head underwater and wearing a mask.

2. Visual angling, where the collector is either submerged with a mask or at least works with a glass-bottomed bucket or from a glass-bottomed boat.

Each method has its advantages and disadvantages.

One species that can be collected with light tackle is *Heniochus acuminatus*. Photo by Ken Lucas.

BLIND ANGLING

"Blind" angling permits collection of species which may not be collected in any other way. In very turbid conditions or in strong surf where diving is out of the question, a well-placed baited hook can produce nice specimens. On the other hand, when it is clear and calm and the collector cannot swim and dive or has no underwater vision, it may be that many undesirables (compared to the few [or no] desired specimens) are taken. Large, strong and hungry fish can time and time again break the delicate lines or engulf the baited hooks to the annoyance of the collector.

In such places as Sri Lanka, the professionals use the midrib of a palm, called the "kitul" (*Caryota urens*), as a fishing rod. Dried and well cured, such a rod costs a trifle, has an ultra-sensitive tip and is also surprisingly strong. But any slender fiberglass rod will do just as well. A slender bamboo rod also is quite suitable, cheaper than a fiberglass one and floats, which is important.

Rings, line guides and a reel are hardly necessary. Tie one end of the line firmly to the tip of the rod. At the other, fix as small a hook as you can possibly get with a scrap of lead for a sinker, about 5-6 inches from it.

To fish for the tiny marine specimens "blind" requires some practice. It is quite an art. One's wrist takes time to respond to the very slight but unmistakable tug of a fish taking the bait.

It is important to strike swiftly before the bait is swallowed. Hooked on the lip, an average marine tropical is unhooked easily and released in a container where it suffers some pain and shock. It recovers in a few hours under tank conditions.

If swallowed, the hook is less easy to remove. Use a tiny disgorger. If this does not work, stick the blunt wooden end of a safety match down the gullet in order to engage the tip of the hook. Press down gently. The hook then will be attached to the match. Pull out the match carefully. The fish is yours unhooked and little the worse for wear for its temporary ordeal.

It is best to hold a fish using a soft cotton glove. Never hold it with thumb and forefinger as the professional fishermen do!

Bait such as cuttlefish and squid are good, but any marine worms are excellent.

A good number of professional fishermen north of

Colombo collect marine tropicals for me on the reefs from their primitive outrigger canoes. They fish "blind," but with remarkable results.

From December until March I get as many of the following as I would ever need:

Cephalopholis boenack, Diploprion bifasciatum, large *Heniochus acuminatus, Sargocentron diadema, Bodianus diana,* large *Pomacanthus annularis, Thalassoma lunare, jansenii* and *hebraicum.*

In addition, I am quite often regaled with:

Adult *Amphiprion clarkii* and *sebae,* adult *Coris gaimard,* medium sized *Gnathanodon speciosus,* adult *Apolemichthys xanthurus,* and *Halichoeres bimaculatus.*

Fishermen operating in surfy tide-pools can hook dozens of fine *Kuhlia taeniura* and a few others, like *Abudefduf sordidus,* with great success.

An exceptionally lovely wrasse, *Thalassoma purpureum,* can be collected by "blind" angling techniques only. It prefers shallow, surfy, almost white water by cliffs and alongside reefs where swimmers and divers cannot operate safely.

Angling by night, one is certain to hook several species of squirrelfishes, probably *Sargocentron diadema* and *Myripristis murdjan.* The latter are caught often on gloomy days over reefs from 30 to 70 feet deep.

If you are not an accomplished diver, you still can collect some fishes simply by angling for them. It is fun, the uncertainty of it. Provided you handle your catches with care, releasing those you do not want, you are collecting in a quite satisfactory manner as regards conservation.

VISUAL ANGLING

This is a particularly exciting and entertaining twist to skin-diving or even wading in the shallows in clear water for marines. Once you are hooked on this technique, it is hard to drag yourself away from it. Certainly, visual angling under water is the only effective and foolproof method of taking a few very choice marines.

The best way to angle visually is to be able to stand on the sand or coral bottom, wearing a mask and, if you need it, a snorkel. Choose a spot that is not too sheltered and where you previously observed fishes of your choice in abundance. On tropical coral reefs, wrasses are the usual specimens that visual anglers go for. But a good many others can be tempted by placing suitable bait close to them.

The angling diver-collector should wear sneakers or canvas boots as protection from the coral. The best container for receiving the catch is a perforated plastic canister around which is tied an old auto inner tube to which is attached a line and small anchor. The professional visual angler should take at least two light rods with him and bait in a plastic bag. The spare rods should be

Amphiprion clarkii can be enticed to spawn in the home aquarium. This pair is guarding a clutch of eggs. The tentacles of the anemone also help protect the eggs. Photo by Mella Panzella.

kept ready inside the canister while the one to be used is carried in one hand.

It is best to wade to a strategic spot, then break open an urchin or some mussels or even disturb the corals to attract the inquisitive wrasses. A baited hook should then be placed in their midst. As soon as it is taken, the angler strikes sharply but gently. It is possible to jerk the bait away from an un-wanted fish and place it closer to the one desired. But on and off it is gobbled up by an undesirable fish which is immediately released and seldom, if ever, makes the same mistake again.

A large undesirable fish can wreck the tackle. In such a case, the line is cut away and another used until repairs can be effected.

Try "wrassing" on a tropical coral reef. It is great fun and very lucrative. On a good morning, even on a well-fished reef in southern Sri Lanka, one can collect up to 50 assorted wrasses comprising *Gomphosus varius, Thalassoma lunare, hardwickii, janseni* and *hebraicum, Halichoeres hortulanus* and *marginatus,* and adult *Coris gaimard.* Often the

bait will be robbed by a *Synodus* or a *Paracirrhites forsteri.* Groupers of small size are great bait gobblers and often bust the ultra-light tackle.

Some of the more drab pomacentrids are a nuisance. They steal the bait as often as it is put in the water. Hook one and release it to lessen the trouble.

It is more difficult to strike at a fish which takes your bait if you are swimming, unless your hand is out of the water completely and you have a good length of line. Generally, the fixed line is about as long as the rod itself. Moreover, unless you are working with an assistant in a boat, it is difficult to unhook and place a fish in a floating container while swimming. When wad-ing, you can do the entire job solo.

SCUBA diving with a baited rod presents the ultimate in underwater angling. It is resorted to only in exceptional circumstances. Doing this solo is complicated and difficult. The results are more reward-ing with a buddy.

A seawater proof plastic reel is an advantage when deep angling with SCUBA. You can

keep the line wound and in place until you are ready to use it. Carrying the bait is a prob-lem. You cannot leave it lying around because it is gobbled up at once by inquisitive snappers and groupers. I prepare small cubes of prawn or cuttle fish which I string on a piece of stiff wire. I carry all this in a small plastic bag tied to the rod handle. A small cube of bait is easy to pull off a wire. It is harder to get a hold of when drifting around in a bag.

Try to angle away from too many rocks or corals. The adult *Coris* often come up in fives and sixes on coarse, sandy bottom with a few corals. They are quick to pick at corals or rocks you may overturn for their benefit. Then place your bait, pay out line and move about 6 to 10 ft. away. Pretty soon your bait is taken. *Coris* are swift and have fine eyesight. Reel in swiftly after striking.

A very ticklish job is remov-ing a hook from the mouth of a slippery fellow like a *Coris* without having it escape. It is best to have your partner swim over with a soft net, enclosing the fish in it. Then remove the hook carefully. Stuff your capture into a suitable plastic or aluminum container.

There is another elusive and beautiful fish that can be caught in this manner. It is *Malacanthus.* These fish are always hunting for food over sand or gritty bottoms in deepish water and where there is a current. A *Malacanthus* is a prize catch. Like *Coris,* it is not distressed by a swifter-than-usual ascent to the surface. Nearly all the *Malacanthus* I get are caught by professional angling blind with light tackle over 40 to 60 feet bottoms.

On a good morning "wrassing," or angling for wrasses, can produce several dozen wrasses, including *Thalassoma lunare.* Photo by M.P. & C. Piednoir.

Soporifics-A Last Resort

Whereas unscrupulous collectors in some areas with access to large quantities of drugs have no hesitation in dumping gallons of the stuff over reefs to stun and kill nearly all the fish within a given area, I would use drugs only as a last resort.

The reasons are quite obvious to anyone with a sense of fair play, conservation and sporting instinct. It simply is ruthless to knock out hundreds of fish just to collect those few you need and let the others die or drift away to be gobbled up by predators.

I use drugs very seldom, and only when all else fails, for a few very choice and elusive specimens. Certainly not for any fish which can be collected by the methods already described.

Drugs are expensive and dangerous, if not troublesome to store and carry. If carelessly used, they can cause unnecessary damage to an underwater ecosystem. Moreover, fish stunned or stupefied with drugs are reported to suffer aftereffects, most usually a refusal to eat. This results in death a few days or weeks after confinement in an aquarium.

The most important principles in collecting live fishes with drugs are: 1) to use as little as possible and 2) to remove specimens from contaminated water with the utmost speed.

There are several soporific drugs on the market. The most effective of them (and perhaps the most expensive, too) is Quinaldine. MS 222

and rotenone are the two others popularly in use, but mostly by scientists after rare fishes for killing and subsequent study. Natives use crushed derris roots and the leaves of certain tropical shrubs. But here, too, the effects take time. When they do, the fish is past the stage of recovery.

A soporific drug that is sold in concentrated liquid form is a very corrosive substance indeed. It is soluble only in acetone or a similar solvent. To prepare a stock solution, put an ounce of the concentrated drug in a pound of acetone. Store in a cool place in a dark, well-stoppered glass bottle. When ready to use it in the field, use an ounce of this stock solution to half a gallon of seawater. Put it in a glass or non-acrylic plastic container. An acrylic plastic is disintegrated by the acetone which dissolves it.

Squirting a compound solution at a fish under water is not as simple as it sounds. It takes practice and patience. Roger Lubbock of England, who was a scientific collector-diver specializing in rare, small marines like *Pseudochromis*, used a simple plastic bag tied around a flexible rubber nozzle. He carried this down with the tip of the nozzle blocked with another piece of plastic and a rubber band. When he spotted his quarry, he chased it into a hole. He then removed the stopper, inserted the rubber nozzle and squirted away. In seconds his prey drifted out stunned. He then gleefully popped them into another plastic bag with fresh sea water where they recover completely in a few minutes.

When I first used drugs, I squirted the stuff at *Paracanthurus hepatus* in dense coral at a depth of 50

When Rodney Jonklaas first used drugs on *Paracanthurus hepatus*, it worked like a charm. But drugs are now considered taboo when collecting fishes. Photo by Gerhard Marcuse.

Ptereleotris zebra is difficult to collect without drugs. A small amount of tranquilizer can be squirted into their hole and the fish can then shortly be sucked out with a vacuum. Photo by U. E. Friese.

The fishes that only can be collected with soporofics are adult *Novaculichthys taeniourus* (an elusive beauty), *Nemateleotris magnifica*, and *Ptereleotris evides*. Also, any gobies or blennies which rush into tiny holes and simply vanish and cannot be traced even if dug for immediately.

The technique is to chase such fishes into their holes, but not too violently. Then gently insert the nozzle of your squirter and give them a small dose. Having taken away the nozzle, cover the hole immediately with a transparent glass or plastic bowl. This keeps the drug inside and around the hole. It also prevents the fish from rushing out—perhaps half asleep— recovering, and then dashing away. In a few seconds you will find your prize drifting helplessly in the bowl. Remove the bowl and place your captive in a perforated container as soon as you possible can.

feet. I used a child's squirt-gun. It worked like a charm. In due course the squirt-gun plastic suffered from the acetone and had to be thrown away. I switched to a large, glass syringe and got perfect results. But these are broken easily in boats or underwater unless handled with extreme care. It helps to bind the more vulnerable parts with a strong tape or sticking plaster. Expose only a small section to indicate how much of the solution you have left. A glass syringe is useful because it is pressure resistant and you can use it several times in one

dive until your solution is exhausted.

With a pliable plastic bag, you get decreasingly powerful doses after each squirt. Seawater under pressure rushes in and occupies the volume of the bag when you have squirted out the original, more powerful solution.

After many frustrating hours with my small squirt-gun, I converted it into a huge squirt-gun. This underwater drug bazooka can take down about a half-gallon of soporific solution and give you up to 20 effective squirts. Clumsy, but it works!

Certain triggers (like a small *conspicillum*) are very rare. They hide in coral or rocks which are not readily removed or broken with a small iron ax. Use a soporific solution and you have your prize. The stunned fish relaxes its trigger spines and drifts out groggily.

It all depends on how badly you want your fish and how much time you have to collect it. Remember that, although drug solutions will work every time, the risk of getting a fish that will suffer from the after-effects and not eat in captivity is very real indeed.

As far as possible, use a little at a time for a specific fish or a pair if them. Take care not to affect other animals close by which you do not need.

The Clown Triggerfish (*Balistoides conspicillum*) is rather rare and difficult to collect. Photo by Dr. Gerald R. Allen, Euston Reef, Great Barrier Reef.

Collecting Invertebrates

For the most part, invertebrates are a lot easier to collect alive, easier to store and transport, and easier to keep in captivity than fishes. Little wonder then that the invertebrate craze is growing faster than that for marine tropical fishes. Most people who fail with fishes and console themselves with invertebrates, soon grow fond of them and keep them in preference to fish.

Collecting invertebrates requires much less skill, experience and cunning than collecting fishes. Most invertebrates do not swim at all and, if they do, they are slow and easily overtaken. The easiest to collect are sedentary invertebrates, like corals and anemones. The most difficult are some crustaceans and molluscs.

I hardly need to go into detail about collecting corals. Just break off or pick up a piece of your choice. The same applies to starfish and urchins, but always wear gloves. Many of them sting!

What is most important about collecting sedentary or semi-sedentary invertebrates is their handling and storage immediately after collection. Here again, the idea is to avoid needless destruction and waste. Take only what you need. Pack and handle with care to get the best results.

Let's go through the invertebrates and discuss the best ways and means of collecting them in good shape.

ANEMONES

Many tropical anemones are colorful, hardy and desirable for keeping alive in aquariums. They can take quite a beating until they are finally established.

To collect anemones, try to pick a location where they grow on smooth rocks or dead corals. *Radianthus* are easy to collect if they grow on any smooth object. Swim very quietly toward them. Before they have time to contract their foot muscles to grip the substratum firmly, give each one a smart tap with the inside of your palm, karate fashion. More often than not, it will be detached and float away. Seize it and thrust it into a bag.

Once a *Radianthus* is alarmed and grips the substratum firmly, it is not easily detached without damage. In this case, use your diving knife. Gently pry the foot away from the rock. Then gently pry away the anemone. Try your best not to damage the foot.

Stoichactis anemones are more difficult. If attached to rocks or corals, they usually are firmly fixed to spots under them. This necessitates your raising up the entire rock or piece of coral or breaking a section to reveal the spot where they are fixed. Then get to work with your knife. Use more care than you would with a *Radianthus*.

Some species of *Stoichactis* live in the sand, as do

An anemone will house a whole family of anemonefishes (seen here is *Amphiprion nigripes*) along with other species, in this case *Dascyllus trimaculatus*. Photo by Dr. Herbert R. Axelrod.

him when coming up for air. He came up head-first under an overhanging ledge on which were growing several huge *Radianthus*. His head got into one of them. He surfaced with what looked like a jelly-wig. It rested on his head for a few seconds until he realized what had happened. Then he flung it away with a loud gasp of horror. He scratched and rubbed his scalp for days after that.

Anemones need less water and oxygen than fishes. They can be packed very tightly. But try to put each one in a separate, small bag. Keep it cool and away from direct sunlight until you can establish it in your aquarium.

CORALS

Only the corals with large, visible polyps are worth collecting alive and keeping in aquaria. It is a waste of time and sheer vandalism to demolish quantities of all corals trying to take them back alive.

Try to pick small pieces, say not more than 4 inches in diameter, of any coral you may want which has large polyps. Use a small hammer or abalone iron to pry the coral away from its substratum. Alternatively, chop it out from a larger colony of which it is a part.

Among the most popular of corals are *Goniopora* and *Trachyphyllia*. They grow in isolated colonies on sand or coral bottoms and are collected easily. *Fungia* lives isolated on the sand. They need very special handling as they are quite delicate. *Dendrophyllia* is a beautiful orange-red, large-polyped coral which lives in caves or

Artistic photograph of a diver getting a close look at an Arrow Crab, *Stenorhynchus seticornis*. Photo by Mike Mesgleski.

Discosoma. Sand anemones are always troublesome to collect. It usually is necessary to work with SCUBA. Dig patiently and carefully around the anemones until you are able to locate the piece of buried rock or coral on which it is fixed. Usually it is a small piece. It is best to extract it

with the anemone attached.

Remember that anemones sting and irritate, so use your gloves. Take care not to let them touch the more tender parts of your body. A former diving buddy of mine once went skin-diving at night for groupers and did not take care to see what was above under ledges away from bright light. This one has to be chopped out with a light hammer. They must be kept in separate bags away from direct sunlight, in an aquarium in dim light or under a rock or coral, in order for it to survive.

GORGONIANS

The beautiful sea fans from deep water in the clear Caribbean, Pacific, and Indian Oceans are difficult, if not impossible, to keep. This is by virtue of the very tiny polyps which require very specialized food, water, and temperature control.

From shallower and more turbid tropical waters come a few very small and striking gorgonians, names as yet uncertain, which have found favor with collectors and marine aquarists. These have very large and conspicuous polyps. They are colored a vivid purple-crimson. They grow no more than 20 inches in height and have few branches. They are very easy to collect. They do surprisingly well in aquariums provided they are anchored away from each other and fed with brine shrimp nauplii. The main point to remember when collecting them is to pack each one individually in a slim, long plastic bag. Cover it entirely with water, not even letting the branches touch each other. If this happens the polyps sting each other to death. The branch may die and eventually break off.

STARFISHES

Dozens of species of starfish abound in tropical waters. They are, of course, easy to collect, with the exception of

Various species of tube worms (as well as a number of other invertebrate and vertebrate animals) make their home in live coral. Pieces of this are known in the aquarium trade as "living rock." Photo by Dr. Gerald R. Allen.

Iconaster longimanus is a colorful starfish found in shallow water. Photo by Allan Power.

the infamous crown-of-thorns (*Acanthaster plancki*). This is poisonous and can cause severe pain and subsequent skin eruption to the victim. Besides, few people want to own even a baby crown-of-thorns because they require a constant diet of live corals.

The small starfish, like the bright red *Fromia*, are collected and transported easily. Be sure not to expose a starfish to the air for even a few seconds after collecting or when packing.

They die off if their delicate filtration systems are interrupted with air bubbles. Transfer each one to a separate bag held in the water. As for most invertebrates, use just a little water and oxygen in packing.

Small starfishes, like this *Fromia elegans*, are easily collected and transported. Photo by Allan Power.

The spines of long spined sea urchins (usually species of the genus *Diadema*) are very delicate as well as venomous. Photo by Allan Power.

do is to raise them to expose these nocturnal creatures. They immediately scuttle away in distress because of the light falling on them. Catch each one carefully by hand and transfer it into a small plastic bag underwater.

Crinoids are not as sedentary as you may think. They can get up and "swim." Photo by M. P. & C. Piednoir.

Never pack starfish together. They soon attack each other and foul the water. In a few hours, they are all dead or dying.

URCHINS

Handle most urchins with gloves and with care. Do not handle the deadly poisonous *Diadema* urchins at all.

Urchins, like starfish, must be transferred from container to bag underwater. They must be packed individually to ensure their good condition. Some urchins living in shallow, turbid water may require

The Slate Pencil Urchin, *Heterocentrotus mamillatus*, is very popular with aquarists. Photo by Allan Power.

frequent water changes in their containers until they have expelled all the debris and foul matter inside their systems. Others expel eggs or sperm in distress when collected. They also foul the containers or bags until flushed out. It is best to keep urchins in a floating, perforated container in the sea until they are all clean. This takes from 1 to 4 hours, depending on the location, size, and species of urchin.

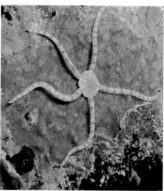

Handle brittle-stars carefully as they are truly "brittle." Photo by Allan Power.

BRITTLE-STARS (OPHIUROIDS)

As their names suggest, they are brittle. Handle them with care. Brittle-stars live under dead coral or rocks in quite shallow water. All you need to

FEATHER-STARS (CRINOIDS)

Feather-stars are very delicate. Yet they are ubiquitous and beautiful. They are easy enough to collect, but are problematical. Their fronds tend to stick to gloves or nets and tear off. This kind of injury seems to be contagious. Pretty soon you have your captive feather-star shedding all its "feathers," looking very pitiful indeed.

The only time I saw feather-stars doing well in captivity was with famous Singaporean diver-collector Jimmy Tan. He had found out that one species, name unknown to me yet, colored a vivid scarlet, could live in an aquarium. Jimmy told me that the best way to handle one is by its tiny feet and not by the feathery arms.

Here again, be sure to pack each crinoid separately in its own plastic bag. Use plenty of water. Ensure that there is minimum variation in temperature and as little jolting as possible to avoid breaking its delicate arms.

Fan worms, like this sabellid worm, are very fast and will disappear even if a shadow passes over them. Photo by Cathy Church.

TUBE-WORMS

Tube-worms are easy to find but not so easy to remove from where they are anchored. The diver should carry a small ax or an abalone iron with which to break open the rocks or coral in which they are anchored. Once fully exposed, the worms in their tubes are pried off easily by hand. Take care not to hurt the delicate tailends.

Calcareous tube-worms are more difficult. Each tube has to be chipped away gently with a hammer or chisel under water taking care not to damage it. The worm will retract in alarm. Be especially careful not to bash the lower portion of the tube.

Tube-worms in their tubes can be packed together temporarily. Like urchins, they exude waste matter for the first few hours, necessitating frequent water changes until they are flushed out.

In the final packing, it is best to put each tube-worm in its own plastic bag. Use enough water to cover it completely and just a little oxygen.

MOLLUSCS

Molluscs have been kept as aquarium pets for years.

Foremost of them is the octopus. We must not forget that nudibranchs, clams and gastropods belong to the same phylum.

The slow movers and sedentary molluscs are easy to collect. The swimmers are difficult in varying degrees.

For sedentary molluscs, like giant clams and fan shells (*Pinna*), it is important to use a sharp knife to cut away the threads, or byssus, attaching the creature to the substratum. Just wrenching out the clam may damage it beyond recovery.

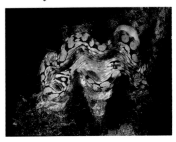

Giant clams (*Tridacna* sp.) will eventually outgrow any but the largest aquaria. Try one of the smaller genera. Photo by Cathy Church.

Burrowing and hiding clams are, of course, much less trouble. Just dig them out or find them by turning over rocks and coral.

It is wise to keep clams in buckets of clean sea water, changing it often to permit the creatures to evacuate themselves by means of their siphons, before packing them in separate bags. All clams are susceptible to fouled water.

Cowries are found under rocks or coral. By day they cover themselves with mantles to protect their lovely shells. When you turn over a rock or coral, be sure to look at the underside carefully for some time—the cowry may reveal

Cowries (*Cypraea* sp.) are favorite molluscs because of their smooth, shiny shells. Photo by Allan Power.

itself. A few cowries, like *Cypraea cribraria*, have vividly colored mantles (this one is a brilliant vermilion red), but most of them have dull, mottled ones which offer more camouflage from predatory fishes.

Cowries never should be packed in large numbers together. They exude slime when in distress and smother each other to death. More importantly, never put small fishes in with live cowries. The fishes are soon in trouble and may not survive because of the slime. In an aquarium, the cowries do not exude slime unless unnecessarily meddled with or distressed. They are best kept away from most fishes.

Conch shells (this is *Strombus gigas*) are adept at puncturing plastic bags. Photo by Courtney Platt.

Strombus, or conch shells, are cute, lively and amusing creatures. They can injure one with their sharp "clawed" feet. They are adept at puncturing plastic bags. Try to put each strombus in its own little bag with perforations. Put several such bags in a big one with water and oxygen. There will be less danger of oxygen and water loss from bag puncture.

As a general rule, try to put each bivalve or univalve mollusc in its own separate bag after collection. You will have less problems, although much more work in the beginning.

Chromodoris quadricolor is one of the nudibranchs or "naked gill" animals. Photo by Allan Power.

Nudibranchs are great favorites. They are caught and kept so easily. Also, they are of small size with so much color. They even can be packed together in pairs if you find them this way. Handle a nudibranch with more care than usual because it is delicate and has no shell for protection.

Baby octopuses are best collected by laying out traps for them. Alternatively, hunt for them in places where natural or artificial traps are already on the sea bottom. Octopuses prefer sandy bottoms with a few hiding places in which to lurk. You

can always spot one by looking for dead shells or crabs and molluscs, and bits and pieces of larger material than usual around their holes.

On a sand bottom in fairly sheltered water, practically any dead gastropod mollusc shell will house a small octopus or a hermit crab. If you have time to lay a series of traps for octopuses, your trouble will be well rewarded. Old tins, coconut shells, ceramic vases—any such object is a temporary home for a young octopus. Just drop them over a suitable bottom and examine them a day or two later, preferably in the morning when the octopuses are resting after their night's foraging. The big problem with octopuses is keeping them in temporary storage. As soon as they are alarmed, and they are nervous, intelligent creatures, they exude ink. This requires an immediate water change and rinsing of the container. An octopus can discharge ink several times in succession. With each emission, the creature grows visibly weaker and paler.

It is absolutely necessary to pack octopuses separately and tie the mouths of the bag firmly. Never keep octopuses with fishes, even for a short time. The fishes are terrified of them.

Enoplometopus debelius is one of the more spectacular crustaceans. Photo courtesy Midori Shobo.

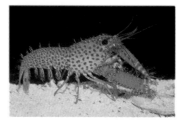

Decorator crabs will attach sponges, algae, or many other animals or plants to their shell for camouflage. Photo by Mike Mesgleski.

CRUSTACEANS

About the most popular of marine invertebrates are members of the class Crustacea—shrimp, crabs, hermit crabs, lobsters, and the like. There are scores of small species which make fine aquarium pets. Most of them are easy to collect, particularly by diving for them. Few are fast enough to evade an average diver with a small net. The main problem is getting them out of holes, cracks, and caves if they creep into them when alarmed.

Let's cite a few of the more popular crustaceans which merit special treatment in collecting techniques.

Stenopus hispidus, the Banded Coral Shrimp, is a cleaner that has a world-wide distribution. Photo by Courtney Platt

The cleaner shrimp, *Stenopus hispidus*, is practically world-wide in distribution in tropical waters. It is about the most popular of all small marine crustaceans for the aquarium. Adults usually are found in pairs in caves and under ledges in quite clear water, and in any depth from 6 ft. to over a hundred. They are slow and trusting. They are not difficult to corner using a small net, but use very fine mesh which does not entangle their pincers. The latter are broken off easily. Although they regenerate, it is nicer to get perfect specimens. The major problem is underwater storage. If you take only two, a pair, per container, they will come out unscathed. However, it is impossible to bring up many of them on a SCUBA dive in one container. They will tear each other to pieces.

It is better to collect one at a time by breath-holding techniques in shallower water. Hand each one to your buddy or boatman. He then must pack it separately in a small bag or put it in a firm plastic box with perforations. These can be floated with others in a

Clown Shrimp, *Hymenocera elegans*, should be kept separately or at most as a pair. Photo by Aaron Norman.

bigger container. The idea is to isolate every specimen before it comes to grips with another and loses its pincers.

Cleaner shrimps are hardy and need little oxygen. You can keep one alive in a few inches of water in a plastic bag for a day. If he sheds, change the water at once and throw away the shed exoskeleton.

The clown shrimp (*Hymenocera elegans*) is a real beauty. It is not so aggressive, but it is better to keep each one separately or just a pair together. They usually are found in pairs under coral ledges. They are gorgeous, gallant little creatures which have been proven to feed on the crown-of-thorns starfish. In an aquarium, they will eat most anything, like shrimp, crab, or fish.

The spectacular barber-pole shrimp or moray-cleaner (*Lysmata grabhami*) lives in water from 30 to 100 feet deep, usually in dark, deep caves in the company of morays. It also seems to like the company of a species of grouper (*Cephalopholis boenack*) in some waters.

The moray-cleaner does just that. When you try to net him with a long-handled net, watch out for hungry or indignant morays! These shrimp are harmless, playful, hardy and gregarious. You can pack

Neopetrolisthes oshimai makes its home in an anemone. Photo by Aaron Norman.

several together without any battling. If they are not fed after more than 24 hours in captivity, they may try to feed on each other.

Many shrimp and crabs live commensally with corals and anemones. They get caught when their homes are collected. They live away from these and eat most any animal food, provided they are protected from fishes. Always pack them separately.

Hermit crabs are easier to find by night than by day. If picking up a big one, mind your fingers! Be sure not to put terrestrial hermit crabs

The diver can see why brittle-stars get their name—three arms have been broken off (but are regenerating!). Photo by Courtney Platt.

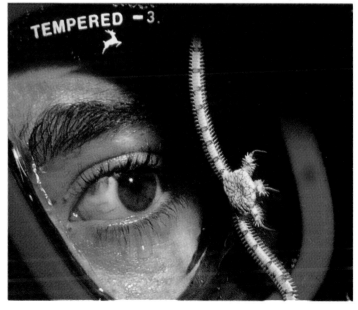

you find on the beaches by night together with aquatic ones. The former will drown.

Most crabs bite. They will bite bags, too. Use a few old bags as liners. Put a new bag around them before filling it with oxygen.

Baby spiny lobsters are not difficult to find and collect. However, never grab them by their long feelers. The technique is to hold a small net with a deep bag in front of the hiding lobster. Then insert a piece of wire behind him and tickle him. He will walk out forwards, turn around and then shoot out swimming backwards, right into your net, and intact. Grabbing the feelers invariably leads to their breaking off. They take a long time to regenerate. Baby lobsters are not quarrelsome. They can be packed together

for some time. When they get hungry, they may pick on the weakest—or the one who has shed its shell—and eat it.

Beware of the mantis shrimp (*Squilla*)! The beautiful, big, tropical squillas are hardy, intelligent and beautiful. They are also bad tempered and powerful. Their rectractile pincers or chelae have knife-like cutting edges. They will slash into anything they resent with the speed and power of a prizefighter.

I have kept several mantis shrimp who have, in sheer rage, smashed aquarium glasses with their chelae. One I netted gave me a terrible wound by striking through the net, the glove and right through a finger in a split second.

If you want a mantis shrimp, use a long-handled

net and strong gloves. Put each one separately in a rigid plastic container. They just tear bags to pieces.

Mantis shrimp live in burrows over sand and near coral. These always have an entrance and an exit. Place your net over one hole and jab away in through the other. Be prepared for a gleaming, high-powered marine mini-locomotive to rush in!

Mantis shrimps always live in deepish water, from 30 to over 100 feet in depth. Some less aggressive species, which live only in deep muddy bottoms, are seldom seen, much less collected, by divers. They also are more delicate and do not last. This is probably because they have been taken in trawler's nets and suffered considerable squeezing with the other catches.

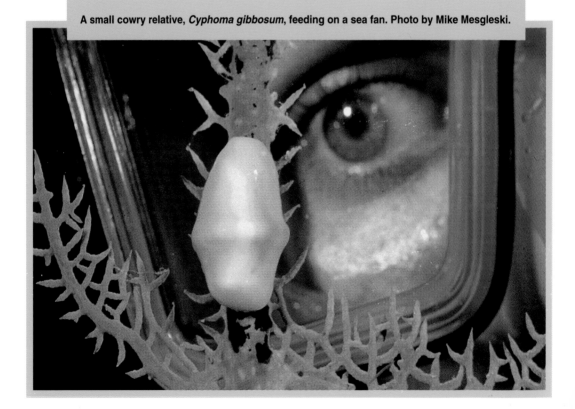

A small cowry relative, *Cyphoma gibbosum*, feeding on a sea fan. Photo by Mike Mesgleski.